# REAL
# LEAN

## Learning the Craft of
## Lean Management

### Bob Emiliani

## Volume Four

The Center for Lean Business Management, LLC
Wethersfield, Connecticut

The Center for Lean Business Management, LLC
Wethersfield, CT
Tel: 860.558.7367     www.theclbm.com

Cover design and page layout by Tom Bittel, bittelworks@sbcglobal.net
www.dadsnoisybasement.com

Library of Congress Control Number:   2008905110
Emiliani, M.L., 1958-
    **REAL LEAN: Learning the Craft of Lean Management
    (Volume Four) / M.L. Emiliani**

Includes bibliographical references and index
1. Business  2. Lean management  3. Leadership

I. Title
ISBN-13:   978-0-9722591-7-0


First Edition     October 2008

ORDERING INFORMATION
www.theclbm.com

Made in the U.S.A. using digital print-on-demand technology.

To those who are
dedicated to their craft.

"I learned from my predecessors to focus on preventing the company from deteriorating to the point where a rescue operation becomes necessary."

\- Fujio Cho
President of Toyota Motor Corporation
*Automotive News*, 19 January 2004

# *Preface*

---

"Learning anything is an act which must be performed by the
learner. It cannot be done for him by the teacher."

- Carl E. Seashore
*Psychology of Music*, 1938, p. 150

The fourth volume of *REAL LEAN* concludes this series of
books. The subtitle of this volume is *Learning the Craft of
Lean Management*. In a sense, this is really what all four volumes have focused on.

Volume One explained the Lean management system in
unique ways to help readers understand Lean as more than just
a "manufacturing thing." Most of the content of Volume Two
compares efforts to promote Scientific Management in the
early 1900s to our efforts to promote Lean management today.
The parallels are striking and we can learn much from the lessons of the past to avoid repeating the same errors. Volume
Three finally answers the question that Lean practitioners have
been asking for decades – "How do you sustain Lean management?" – by dissecting conventional management thinking
and practice which so strongly hinders managers' ability to
become Lean leaders.

Volume Four focuses specifically on understanding Lean management as a craft that executives must practice daily in order
to gain proficiency. It touches upon several important aspects
of the craft, which Lean management practitioners must better
understand if they hope to succeed in their efforts.

All four volumes emphasize the "Respect for People" principle because this principle has been missing from the practice
of Lean management. This is this principle that makes Lean
management work, and so it must never be ignored.

My purpose in writing and publishing these books is to help
people to better understand Lean management. Books are an
effective, easy to distribute, low cost way to learn – provided
somebody reads them (hopefully more than once).

However, reading by itself is never enough, especially when it
comes of Lean management. Senior managers must go to the
"gemba," the place where the work is actually performed, to
understand the work and participate in improvement activities.
Doing this allows them to apply what they have learned from
reading books, and, over time, they become much smarter and
more capable leaders.

Yucika Kalvari, an emerging Lean leader from Indonesia, said
it well when he noted the importance of books as part of the
process for learning Lean management:

> "I understand that gemba is important in learning, but
> I want to integrate book study and experience. By
> reading books you can reach something beyond your
> experience, by experiencing what you read you reach
> the next stage of your understanding. And like a cir-
> cle, you can sharpen your understanding from experi-
> ence by reading what other people say about in books.
> I always search books that are written by authors who
> have experience in the area and whose ideas have

proven to be effective. I personally have the opportunity to be a Lean leader because I read. My personal
experience with books is that even if I have no hands-
on experience in Lean, I was ready to experience it
when the opportunity arose because I had already
gained the fundamental knowledge."

The integration of book study and experience is an excellent
approach. It can be greatly improved upon by learning directly from other people who have learned the craft of Lean management. However, such persons do not exist in most companies, so the approach Yucika Kalvari is taking is logical and
practical. Just make sure, as Yucika does, that the books you
choose "are written by authors who have experience in the
area and whose ideas have proven to be effective."

It is ironic how Lean management, designed to move beyond
both craft and mass production, is itself a craft that can only be
learned just as any other craftsman [1] would learn their trade:
observation, daily practice, small-scale experimentation, reading, dialogue, feedback, and other practical ways to learn.

The challenge we face is to get senior managers to understand
that their chosen profession, management, is a craft, not a simple activity that they can improvise. Craft work requires thousands of hours of practice to gain proficiency, which can only
be done through direct participation in continuous improvement activities and also through the application of Lean principles and practices to managers' own day-to-day work.

Despite senior managers' stated commitment to continuous
improvement, most prefer to stick to their practice of conven-

tional management that they learned long ago. They have yet to learn the management craft that is consistent with the outcomes that they seek: greater customer satisfaction, increased market share, new products, better financial and non-financial performance, etc. That craft is Lean management.

I sincerely hope that readers find this volume, and the entire series of *REAL LEAN* books, helpful in expanding their knowledge of the Lean management system, and that their daily practice strengthens and improves. I also hope these four volumes help convince readers that Lean management is low risk and offers very high rewards – but only to those who are willing to learn the craft.

Finally, my tone in this volume is very direct, just as it is in my other books. Please do not be offended by my sharp comments. My intent is simply to lay facts bare and help executives improve.

Bob Emiliani
September 2008
Wethersfield, Conn.

[1] The word "craftsman" is used in this book as a gender-neutral term, meaning man or woman.

# *Contents*

# *Prologue*

Volumes One through Four of the *REAL LEAN* books series has sought to accomplish many things for readers. Foremost among them is to map the current state of Lean management, in words, at the start of the twenty-first century, some 30 years after people became aware of Toyota's management system.

If you have read the first three volumes you might come away with the view that the glass is half-empty with respect to the progress that has been achieved thus far and the long-term prospects for Lean management. Actually, the glass is more than half-empty. This reflects the fact, the reality, that there are very few companies that do Lean correctly – meaning, the practice of both principles: "Continuous Improvement" and "Respect for People" [1].

The historical record is very clear regarding Lean and its antecedents: most executives do not understand Lean or eventually fail even after having experienced some success. Hence, there is perhaps one business in 100 that today practices Lean correctly – despite the enormous amount of knowledge of progressive management practices that have accumulated over the last century. While knowledge has certainly accumulated, it is apparent that know-how has not.

The fact that the glass is more than half-empty should not discourage anyone. Even one percent of a large number, such as the number of companies that exist world-wide, is still a big number. What is most important is to see reality as it actually is; doing so is a critical, fundamental capability in Lean management. Look at the facts and see the reality as it is, no matter how ugly the current state is, respond to it, evaluate the results, and make improvements – the plan-do-check-act (PDCA) cycle.

This current state map of Lean management establishes the baseline from which we must improve. Lean will not advance as a management system if we ignore the current state. The fact that the Lean community struggles to understand why so many companies, and the senior managers that lead them, have such great difficulty understanding and correctly practicing Lean management indicates that it is not acknowledging the current state. This means that the strategies and tactics that have been used to advance Lean may be inadequate, incomplete, or flawed. We need to think more about what we are doing if we expect to realize a desirable future state.

The current state map suggest there are a few fundamental factors that put Lean management out of reach of all but the few, most dedicated presidents and CEOs. If something as good as Lean management, with its well-documented wide-ranging benefits to key stakeholders – suppliers, employees, customers, investors, and communities – cannot substantially displace or even effectively compete against conventional management, then Lean itself must suffer from one or more serious problems.

To put it bluntly, is Lean the Betamax of management systems? This superior, mid-1970s, videotape recording format never gained a large commercial market share. It appealed mainly to high-end industrial users and schools. Perhaps Lean management is destined to have only a small market share like Betamax, mainly among egghead presidents and CEOs.

After all, it makes sense that the "Thinking Management System" [2] would have greatest appeal to presidents and CEOs who think. These people are the connoisseurs of management who love to learn new things and put innovations into practice.

We should never lose sight of the fact that conventional management is super-sticky. It apparently gives senior managers a better experience with regard to power and control. It offers more opportunities to be a hero. Peers in the business community accept conventional management and it is consistent with what they learned in college and graduate school. It confirms many flawed assumptions including business as being complex and that they are the boss, not their customers. For these and other reasons, the current state is very persistent.

After nearly 15 years of practicing Lean management, observing executives practice Lean, and extensive study of the history of Lean and the management systems from which it evolved, it is apparent that Lean management suffers from three serious, fundamental problems:

<u>1. Lean cannot move beyond its narrow characterization as an operating practice.</u>

For over 30 years people have pigeon-holed Lean as a better way to manage operations and have not understood it as a better way to manage the entire company. It is true that this view has finally begun to change in some corporations that have embraced Lean more broadly. But they are few in number, there is usually less than 100 percent buy-in among senior managers, and their knowledge of the nuances of Lean management and interconnections between the "Continuous Improvement" and "Respect for People" principles remains very poor.

Recently, the Lean community has begun to move away from the phrase "Lean manufacturing." However, instead of calling it "Lean management," many now commonly refer to it as "operational excellence." This new phrase essentially keeps Lean in the same tiny box it has long occupied. Executives who are not responsible for operations will most likely continue to ignore Lean – meaning 9 out of 10 executives in a senior management team will, for the most part, ignore Lean.

Lean often does not work to senior management's satisfaction even when it is narrowly applied as an operating practice. So, you better believe that most executives will not consider Lean more broadly as a management system. They will instead look for something else, the next big thing, to help them meet business objectives.

The Lean community must realize that the clock is ticking. We can reasonably expect two or three generations of managers, Baby Boomers to Generation X [3], to pursue Lean management. After that, subsequent generations will likely perceive Lean management as "old and tired." Most Generation Y and Generation Z workers are today being exposed to ill-conceived and poorly executed Lean management (Fake Lean). Lean could become "your father's Oldsmobile" to them, making it unlikely that they would want to practice Lean management when they become senior managers in 10 or 20 years.

History, not surprisingly, is repeating itself. Between about 1900-1940, executives persistently viewed Scientific Management [4] as an operating practice and not as a management system as its creators intended it to be. After about 30 years, interest in Scientific Management began to wane. Scientific Management ceased to exist as a management system shortly after World War II, but parts of it lived on as cherry-picked tools to improve operations [5, 6]. Scientific Management became "your father's Oldsmobile" to the post-World War II whiz kid executives born of the Greatest Generation.

### 2. Too difficult to understand and apply the "Respect for People" principle.

Most managers are unaware of the "Respect for People" principle, but they should not be. If only they were to think and analyze the root cause of backslide and continuous improvement efforts that fail, they would quickly realize what the problems are and that the key countermeasure is "Respect for People."

Managers who have heard about the "Respect for People" principle think they know what it means, but most do not, and therefore they apply this principle superficially at best. Nearly all have too narrow a view of the "Respect for People" principle, where people refers only to employees. In fact, it refers to employees, suppliers, customers, shareholders, and communities. Others think the "Respect for People" principle is optional, or they can let it slide and nobody will notice. Well, people do notice.

The "Respect for People" principle is not optional in Lean

management – it is required [1, 7, 8]. It is what makes Lean management work and gives it its unique and desirable non-zero-sum (win-win) characteristics. But sadly, this principle is much too difficult to understand given that it is infinitely easier for executives to comprehend and practice zero-sum (win-lose) conventional management.

Again, history is repeating itself. A direct predecessor of Lean management also stressed the importance of "Respect for People," characterized at the time as "cooperation" between management and workers, but was ignored by the vast majority of executives [5].

### 3. Changes in company leadership severely disrupt or destroy Lean.

If a company manages to dodge the first two problems, this third one will almost surely get them. It is a fact that managers come and go; they retire, get better offers, pass away, etc., and companies are bought and sold. If the people who are promoted, hired, or inserted into new senior management positions know nothing about Lean – or think they know, but don't – then they will quickly drive the company back to conventional, pedestrian, zero-sum management practices and metrics [7]. Realistically, you cannot expect anything more because that is truly all they know.

Once again, this recurring problem is found throughout the history of progressive management (e.g. Ford's management system and Taylor's Scientific Management) [5].

For Lean management to survive long-term in a company,

there has to be continuity in senior management and promotion from within of people who are among the most skilled practitioners of Lean management. Executives have to respect the next generation of managers and transfer their accumulated Lean knowledge and skills to them – the know-how.

It is a long-term commitment to learn the Lean management system, with outstanding results steadily achieved along the way if it is practiced correctly. Under any circumstance, senior managers must do some "Lean enterprise estate planning" [9] to help sustain the management system long-term.

Many other issues are embedded within each of the three problems cited, such as: a strong tendency among senior managers to cherry-pick Lean tools, focus on doing things and not on balancing thinking and doing, little desire to practice Lean every day, confusion over corporate purpose, the absence of business principles, and flawed economics.

So what can we do about these three problems and other factors that undercut Lean management's ability to displace conventional management? I have analyzed these problems in detail and suggested several courses of action and practical countermeasures in previous writings [6, 10-11]. But still, something important is missing.

What we have clearly failed to do is inform presidents and CEOs of how much their conventional management practice, loaded with waste (muda) [12], unevenness (mura), and unreasonableness (muri), costs the company.

Most executives are numbers-driven. Maybe they need to see

some numbers to wake them up to the opportunity and propel them to adopt Lean as the management system, not as an operating practice. So what do waste, unevenness, and unreasonableness cost a business? I estimate it to be as follows for a manufacturing business:

$$C_{WUU} = I + 0.3 \ F + 0.3 \ DL + 0.5 \ IL$$

Where,

I = Inventory, the dollar value of inventory; sum of raw material, work-in-process, and finished goods in excess of 30 days. The assumption is that 12 inventory turns would be a minimum level of "Lean-ness." Obviously, the goal is more than twelve turns, but this simply establishes a baseline for the estimate.

F = Facilities cost, the annual occupancy cost of shop and office space. It is well known that in a Lean transformation that there is approximately 30 percent excess shop and office area [13].

DL = Direct labor, the annual cost of direct labor plus benefits. It is well known that prior to a Lean transformation that there is approximately 30 percent more direct labor than is needed for current sales volumes [13].

IL = Indirect labor, annual cost of indirect labor plus benefits, including executive pay and benefits. On average, indirect labor is only 50 percent productive in an eight hour day [14]. Their time, which the company pays for, is wasted due to: organizational politics, unknown expectations, poor direction, too many projects, lack of focus, re-work, processes not defined/ill-defined, bogus corporate initiatives, gaming the metrics, cover-your-ass reports, preparing presentations, firefighting, budgeting/re-budgeting, and other unassignable nonsense.

Please note that over-hiring is management's fault and should not be addressed through involuntary layoffs because this would violate the "Respect for People" principle. The excess labor represents a big opportunity to grow the business, which all presidents and CEOs say they want to do [15].

Here is a sample calculation for a manufacturing business with $3.5 billion in annual sales and a cost of goods sold of $2.4 billion:

Inventory = $500 million at 4.8 inventory turns, so excess
   I = $300 million
Facilities Cost = $500 million
Direct Labor = $300 million
Indirect Labor = $700 million

$$C_{WUU} = 300 + 0.3(500) + 0.3(300) + 0.5(700) = \$890,000,000 \text{ est.}$$

The estimated cost of waste, unevenness, and unreasonableness is $890,000,000, or 25 percent of sales. That's a big number!

Remember, this is an estimate. However, my Lean accounting friends tell me that the "Emiliani Method" for calculating waste, unevenness, and unreasonableness is in the ballpark.

What does waste, unevenness, and unreasonableness cost a service business? It is the same equation, but substitute 0.5

GM for I, inventory, where GM is the gross margin. The rationale is that a Lean business should generate 50 percent more gross margin than a conventionally managed business because it is better at serving end-use customers' needs.

The estimated cost of waste, unevenness, and unreasonableness should be a bit more than 25 percent of sales because service business productivity is generally lower than manufacturing business productivity.

The significance of this back-of-the-envelope calculation is as follows:

> Conventional management is just too expensive for any company or organization to use. Further, managing a business using conventional management is fiscally irresponsible. It is inconsistent with the fiduciary and other responsibilities of the officers of the company. **The case for REAL LEAN management is crystal clear.**

The numbers are so big that they should motivate a larger population of executives to want to adopt Lean management because they are usually bottom line and shareholder-focused. Recognizing this might give Lean a greater share of the management system market and raise it above the level of a niche product. In addition, shareholders and other key stakeholders should demand that executives use a less resource-intensive management system – Lean management.

Calculating the estimated cost of waste, unevenness, and unreasonableness does not provide any defense against the three fundamental problems mentioned previously. The only defense is to correctly understand and apply Lean principles and practices, and plan for the long-term.

That means to learn the craft of Lean management. So please read on.

**Notes**

[1] "The Toyota Way 2001," Toyota Motor Corporation, internal document, Toyota City, Japan, April 2001

[2] Teruyuki Minoura, "Address to the World Class Manufacturing Forum," May 2002, http://www.electronics-scotland.com/industry_comment/comment_item.cfm?itemID=18

[3] See Wikipedia, "List of Generations," http://en.wikipedia.org/wiki/List_of_generations

[4] F.W. Taylor, *The Principles of Scientific Management*, Harper & Brothers Publishers, New York, NY, 1911

[5] B. Emiliani, *REAL LEAN: Critical Issues and Opportunities in Lean Management*, Volume Two, The CLBM,

LLC, Wethersfield, Conn., 2007, Chapters 1-4 and 10

[6] B. Emiliani, *REAL LEAN: The Keys to Sustaining Lean Management*, Volume Three, The CLBM, LLC, Wethersfield, Conn., 2008

[7] B. Emiliani, with D. Stec, L. Grasso, and J. Stodder, *Better Thinking, Better Results: Case Study and Analysis of an Enterprise-Wide Lean Transformation*, second edition, The CLBM, LLC, Wethersfield, Conn., 2007, pp. 283-290

[8] J. Liker and M. Hoseus, *Toyota Culture*, McGraw-Hill, New York, NY, 2008

[9] B. Emiliani, *REAL LEAN: Critical Issues and Opportunities in Lean Management*, Volume Two, The CLBM, LLC, Wethersfield, Conn., 2007, Chapter 13

[10] B. Emiliani, *REAL LEAN: Critical Issues and Opportunities in Lean Management*, Volume Two, The CLBM, LLC, Wethersfield, Conn., 2007

[11] B. Emiliani, *Practical Lean Leadership: A Strategic Leadership Guide for Executives*, The CLBM, LLC, Wethersfield, Conn., 2008

[12] Where waste refers to the eights wastes: defects, transportation, overproduction, waiting, processing, movement, inventory, and (leadership) behaviors. See T. Ohno, *Toyota Production System: Beyond Large-Scale Production*, Productivity Press, Portland, OR, 1988, pp. 19-20 and M.L. Emiliani, "Lean Behaviors," *Management Decision*, Vol. 36, No. 9, pp. 615-631, 1998

[13] B. Emiliani, with D. Stec, L. Grasso, and J. Stodder, *Better Thinking, Better Results: Case Study and Analysis of an Enterprise-Wide Lean Transformation*, second edition, The CLBM, LLC, Wethersfield, Conn., 2007

[14] Bob Emiliani, unpublished research.

[15] There are exceptions. Presidents and CEOs of small businesses often do not want to grow.

# 1 Ten Thousand Hours

*Executives who view Lean management as merely a source of explicit knowledge embodied in Lean tools and processes, applied by people in lower levels of the organization, will never realize much success because they lack critically important tacit knowledge that can only come from direct participation in the application of Lean principles and practices. Lean management is itself a craft that can only be learned the old-fashioned way, just as any other craftsman would learn their trade: observation, daily practice, small-scale experimentation, reading, dialogue, and feedback.*

Researchers have long studied craftsmen [1] to better understand what it takes to learn the requisite skills and to become successful practitioners of quality-driven work. They are also very interested to know how long it takes to gain proficiency in a craft. The answer they get is usually the same: about 10,000 hours [2]. That's how long it takes to gain both the explicit knowledge (knowledge documented in the form of work instructions, procedures, etc. – the "science") and tacit knowledge (knowledge that is unspoken, implied, or learned through experience – the "tricks of the trade" or the "art") to learn a craft.

Whether the craft is visual arts, writing, music, textiles, woodworking, or metalworking, it takes about 10,000 hours of daily training to gain a solid foundation of capabilities to further build upon. The craftsman labors long hours pursuing the dream of becoming a skilled practitioner who can earn a living from the craft.

For musicians, this means practicing four hours a day, every day, for about seven years. That's what it takes to become proficient at playing an instrument, knowing how to read music well, and how to perform with others. People who commit to learning their craft are willing to make thousands of errors early in their training to avoid costly errors in the future. While this may seem inefficient in the short-term, it is very efficient in the long-term. Error-free work is a hallmark of good craft.

In contrast, managers learning conventional management are discouraged from making errors because errors are viewed as bad in a business setting. They are willing to avoid errors early in their careers, only to make many errors later in their careers – often very costly errors. While this may seem efficient in the short-term, it is horribly inefficient in the long-term. There is no craftsmanship when errors are common.

In the business world you can easily find dozens of major errors in management thinking and practice [3]. These errors recur over time and are better characterized as "durable errors." They exist because some leaders may be unaware of them, while other leaders are unwilling to correct durable errors for fear of looking stupid, admitting fault, making their predecessor look bad, etc.

In addition, top managers often mistakenly assume the errors are expensive to fix, will take too long to fix, or both. So they just accept the errors and rationalize them by saying: "nothing is perfect" or "people will always make errors." Durable errors are evidence of very low quality management work and insincere commitment to continuous improvement among executives.

Not surprisingly, it takes about 10,000 hours to learn conventional management. In a 2,000 hour work year, much of what we learn about conventional management takes place in the first five years at work. Most executives would not view their first five years at work as 10,000 hours of daily on-the-job training in conventional management practice. But that is what it is.

While we may not become a supervisor or manager until some years later, what we learn about conventional management comes from observing how things get done and by participating in established processes. We assume the processes must be good, if a little quirky, because: "we are a successful, profitable company," or "the process has been in place for a long time, so it must be OK."

New hires tend to be quite accepting of the current state in their first five years in the workplace. Their faulty assumptions and acceptance of the way things are turn out to be big barriers to learning the craft of Lean management later on when they become mid-level managers and executives.

Take organizational politics, for example. This is a low-quality form of human interaction in the workplace that undercuts leadership, quality, and craftsmanship. Organizational politics introduces defects, delays, and rework, disrupts material and information flows, and creates no value for end-use customers. Yet most executives accept wasteful, zero-sum organizational politics as a necessary evil; that it must be managed because it cannot be eliminated [4]. Steadfast adherence to this view becomes a huge barrier to learning the craft of Lean management.

It also takes about 10,000 hours of daily training to gain a solid foundation of capabilities to practice the craft of Lean management. That seems like a big commitment. Most executives will say that they do not have time for that (a bad assumption), which helps explain why they delegate Lean implementation to lower level people (a critical error in judgment).

Executives cannot learn a craft by delegating the work to others. It would be like striving to become a skilled carpenter by delegating the actual task of woodworking to someone else while the boss reads a book about carpentry or learns about woodworking from a computer simulation. Executives must instead directly participate in the application of Lean principles and practices to simultaneously develop the explicit and tacit knowledge in real-time. Learning Lean management requires engaging both the brain and hands. Disconnecting the two and thinking that all that is needed are the "brains," the explicit knowledge, is a common fundamental error.

The workplace provides opportunities every minute of every day for executives to apply Lean principles and practices. In a 2,000 hour work year, it will take executives about five years to learn the foundation of the craft of Lean management [5]. But they can only learn it by participating in continuous improvement activities that use Lean tools and processes, and also by applying Lean principles and practices to their own day-to-day work activities. In addition, all managers must simultaneously practice the "Respect for People" principle [6], which has long been the biggest challenge in Lean management [7].

Let's not forget that once you learn a craft, you have to keep practicing it daily to strengthen and improve your understanding and skills. Failure to practice will quickly lead to backslide.

Perhaps an analogy will be helpful to describe what it is like to transition from practicing conventional management to practicing Lean management. It is akin to going from painting, which is two-dimensional, to sculpture, which is three-dimensional. Some of what an artist learns from painting will be useful and can be applied to sculpture, but sculpture is a different craft. Sculpture operates by different aesthetic principles, utilizes different tools and processes, and has different rules which require thousands of hours of additional training to gain proficiency.

Conventional management is approximately 80 percent explicit knowledge and 20 percent tacit knowledge. Lean management is the opposite; about 80 percent tacit knowledge and 20 percent explicit knowledge. That is a huge difference, and illustrates why most managers fail to grasp Lean management. They think Lean is just like conventional management in terms if the amount of explicit and tacit knowledge. That assumption is incorrect.

Explicit knowledge is often viewed by executives as the more important of the two types of knowledge [8]. The assumption that explicit knowledge is superior, or more authoritative, usually prevails. While explicit knowledge is certainly necessary, it is not sufficient. Tacit knowledge must not be discounted because it is equally important. That is why, for example, many outsourcing projects turn into disasters. People who do the outsourcing possess all the necessary explicit knowledge, but success depends on tacit knowledge which they lack.

Similarly, that is why most Lean transformations don't succeed. Senior managers my have read a book and gained some explicit knowledge, but they have not put in the personal time and effort necessary to learn the tacit knowledge – e.g. the correct use and meaning of Lean tools and processes, and how they relate to Lean principles. This is all-important in Lean management.

In addition to formal and on-the-job training, Toyota has always had a parent-child approach for management training (similar to the craftsman-apprentice relationship), which reflects senior management's understanding of Lean as a craft. Specifically, the transmittal of both explicit and tacit Lean knowledge from one generation of managers to the next. Retired Toyota executive Teruyuki Minoura explains it as follows [9]:

> "The transmission of a fundamental philosophy to new people or to the next generation is… [a process called] 'ikusei.' This concept is closer to 'nurturing or raising,' just as parents raise children, than to simple education or training. Parents raise children through instruction, training, and by setting examples day in and day out. That is what we must do at Toyota, to instill our core philosophies as well as the practical know-how of the Toyota Production System… Training and learning are parts of a life-long process

that never cease as long as one works for Toyota…
Toyota managers are expected to train and nurture
their subordinates, just as parents raise their children."

Ultimately, learning the craft of Lean management is fun and
much more rewarding. It creates better leaders because they
can satisfy customers and achieve business objectives without
having to rely on primitive zero-sum (win-lose) tactics. Such
tactics represent a low level of leadership capability; that of
an amateur (Figure 1a [10]).

Lean leads to a higher level of leadership capability that all
executives who consider themselves "professional" should
want to strive for – the level of a craftsman (Figure 1b [11]).
The craftsman focuses on the work, not the reward.
Executives must do good quality management work, free of
durable errors and other types of problems that needlessly

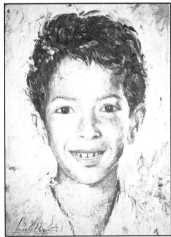

Figure 1a                    Figure 1b

consume resources [12]. From that the rewards will come. In addition, they will learn valuable lessons on limits that must be acknowledged and major opportunities that have long gone unrecognized.

The next step, for a few Lean leaders, is to become virtuosos. However, both craftsmen and virtuoso Lean leaders must also be teachers who teach every day to train the next generation of apprentice Lean leaders and also document what they have learned.

**Notes**

[1] The word "craftsman" is used in this book as a gender-neutral term, meaning man or woman. It is synonymous with the word "artisan."

[2] D. Levitin, *This is Your Brain on Music*, Plume Penguin Group, New York, NY, 2006, pp. 197-198

[3] M.L. Emiliani, "Standardized Work for Executive Leadership," *Leadership and Organizational Development Journal*, Vol. 29, No. 1, pp. 24-46, 2008

[4] By having the attitude that organizational politics is a necessary evil, top executives set the bar very low for themselves and their direct reports. In doing so, they reveal their willingness to live with mountains of behavioral waste (see M.L. Emiliani, "Lean Behaviors," *Management Decision*, Vol. 36, No. 9, pp. 615-631, 1998). In classical economics, taxes are also seen as a necessary evil (to pay for roads, for example), but which causes distortions and reduces economic efficiency. Likewise, organizational politics functions as a tax on an organization in that it, too, causes distortions and also reduces corporate operating (and non-operating) efficiency – particularly the interactions between human beings who are the conduits (or blockades) for material and information flows. The economic efficiency of organizations is reduced by zero-sum organizational politics (blame, in particular). Thus, instead of fomenting organizational politics, top management should seek to reduce and even eliminate it (see B. Emiliani, *Practical Lean Leadership: A Strategic Leadership Guide for Executives*, The CLBM, LLC, Wethersfield, Conn., 2008).

[5] B. Emiliani, with D. Stec, L. Grasso, and J. Stodder, *Better Thinking, Better Results: Case Study and Analysis of an Enterprise-Wide Lean Transformation*, second edition, The CLBM, LLC, Wethersfield, Conn., 2007

[6] "The Toyota Way 2001," Toyota Motor Corporation, internal document, Toyota City, Japan, April 2001

[7] B. Emiliani, *REAL LEAN: The Keys to Sustaining Lean Management*, Volume Three, The CLBM, LLC, Wethersfield, Conn., 2008, Appendix I, "The Equally Important 'Respect for People' Principle," pp. 121-137

[8] Further, being a quick study with respect to explicit knowledge is regarded as a sign of great leadership capability and future potential. This is a mistake. Executives must learn both the explicit and tacit knowledge the hard way, as craftsmen do.

[9] T. Minoura, "Address to the World Class Manufacturing Forum," May 2002,http://www.electronics-scotland.com/industry_comment/comment_

item.cfm?itemID=18. In that same speech, Minoura had this to say about Toyota management's view of craftsmanship: "...when we talk about 'mono-zukuri' at Toyota, it is more than just manufacturing. It involves the idea of creating a product. It implies a love of creation. It also encompasses the sense of craftsmanship. Making and crafting a product with expertise and with high quality."

[10] *Daddy (Mario)*, Michael Emiliani, ink on canvas board, 1995. Used with permission.

[11] *Mario (Son)*, Lester de Quirós, oil on canvas, 1968

[12] B. Emiliani, *Practical Lean Leadership: A Strategic Leadership Guide for Executives*, The CLBM, LLC, Wethersfield, Conn., 2008

# 2 Learn Lean When Times are Good

*When do top executives adopt Lean management? Usually, it's when times are tough. Why do top executives adopt Lean management? To reduce costs, improve profitability, and increase the stock price. This reasoning is totally incorrect and contributes to the many failed Lean transformations that we have witnessed over the last 30 years. So when should management adopt Lean management and what is the right reason for doing so?*

Executives should adopt Lean when times are good and not when times are bad, as they normally do. Adopting Lean management when times are bad is like a student cramming the night before a test. They should have been studying all along, but instead procrastinated and failed to manage their responsibilities and meet commitments.

We all know that cramming for tests yields poor results. Likewise, cramming to adopt Lean management in a year or two because business conditions have deteriorated is not going to succeed. But that won't stop executives from trying to lessen the impact of an economic downturn. Truly, I wish them well, but they should not wait until circumstances become dire.

The odds are against executives who adopt Lean when the economy is poor. In fact, the failure rate is nearly 100 percent. The reason is that Lean management is not a simple addition of new Lean knowledge to executives' existing base of conventional management knowledge. Adopting Lean means that conventional management knowledge and practices must be removed and replaced with Lean principles and practices. This replacement process requires learning new things over an extended period of time, just as it takes an extended period of time to learn conventional management.

Most executives will not do this when times are tough. Instead, they will reflexively rely on what they already know how to do, and they will add a little bit of Lean – mostly the application of some cherry-picked Lean tools to improve short-term operating performance and reduce costs. They will surely resort to layoffs, many of which will not be needed, and workers will view layoffs as having been directly caused by Lean. Management's actions will quickly kill all enthusiasm for Lean among workers and supervisors. They won't behave like Lean leaders because they do not possess the beliefs of Lean leaders.

The leaders of the Lean community have done a pitiful job over the last 30 years, and particularly the last 20 years, of informing executives about the "Respect for People" principle in Lean management [1] and protecting workers from harm. This principle has been hidden in plain view for decades, but has only recently become a subject for discussion [2]. It should have been the main subject of discussion from the start because of executives' consistent, long-term pattern of behavior, since the 1880s, which is to lay people off after process improvements have been achieved [3].

The failure to acknowledge this reality, identify root causes, and implement practical countermeasures means that many people will get laid off as a result of Lean when economic conditions deteriorate. We lose the opportunity to prevent each new round of human suffering by spending too much time focusing on the application of Lean tools, such as value stream maps and creating value stream managers, to improve operating efficiency. The approach to implementing Lean has long been narrow and unbalanced. This is a repetitive error.

So what can we do? The reality is that we are not prepared to respond to the problems we now face. Broadly speaking, Lean community leaders are too deeply invested in comprehending Lean narrowly as just tools for managers' tool kits. They are not yet able to articulate Lean as a management system consisting of two principles: "Continuous Improvement" and "Respect for People," what "Respect for People" means, and especially how these two principles interact with each other [4].

We could, together, try to quickly swing the pendulum in the opposite direction, for a limited time, and teach executives that Lean is a human-centered management system that is congruent with corporate fiscal responsibility [5] and ethical behavior towards its stakeholders (employees, suppliers, customers investors, and communities). In other words, Lean management, practiced properly, has the ability to greatly strengthen fiscal and ethical responsibility in a manner that cannot be achieved in any other way [6]. This will address executives' concerns about the long-term success of the business.

But what about the short-term, which executives will surely be more focused on? One thing is certain: executives make a lot mistakes when they are immersed in a crisis. Many of the decisions they make will marginalize the interests of key stakeholders in the name of ensuring the company's survival. Stakeholders who have been marginalized will be less motivated to help the company out of the crisis and will surely remember the unkind actions they suffered. No doubt, most will find a way to get even when economic conditions improve. However, these costly tit-for-tat behaviors are not a given; it does not have to be that way.

Given the plethora of short-term business problems created by a downturn or a recession, Lean management could be used to promote widespread collaboration among stakeholders to identify and correct thousands of short-term problems that affect everyone in some way or another. Instead of one stakeholder winning and other stakeholders losing (zero-sum), all stakeholders win (non-zero-sum) – maybe not as much as they would like, but they will be satisfied with outcomes that are fair. In other words, put the "Respect for People" principle into practice immediately and with genuine conviction – within the company and between the company and its stakeholders.

Lean management can help executives weather an economic storm with fewer mistakes and also be better prepared for when business conditions improve.

However, if Lean management is adopted by executives because of poor economic conditions and is practiced in the usual zero-sum manner – for example, laying off workers who have improved processes or using reverse auctions to squeeze suppliers [7] – then this will strengthen the already negative perceptions that many people have of Lean. This will make it even more difficult to convince executives and workers of the merits of Lean management when business conditions improve.

Indeed, pervasive misapplication of Lean management will further damage Lean, perhaps to the point where it is no longer relevant to most executives.

This would be an unfortunate outcome because Lean management will always be relevant to the cooperative human-economic activity known as "business." Why? It is because Lean management, practiced in a non-zero-sum fashion, helps a business compete better in every process and every activity. That's why executives should adopt Lean management.

Lean management has numerous unique advantages compared to conventional management, all of which executives should seek if they are sincere about fulfilling their duties as officers of the company. These advantages include:

- Better way to align management system with buyers' market and grow [8]
- Create flow [9]
- Improve fiscal responsibility, as well as financial and non-financial performance
- Develop human resources
- Simplify the business and improve reliability
- See reality clearly so that people can respond to it

While the timing and rationale for adopting Lean is often poor, it is nevertheless a point of entry into a better way to manage and to satisfy customers. What the Lean management system offers to executives is a proven way to deal with economic turmoil, in ethical and fiscally responsible ways, with fewer mistakes, and strengthen overall competitiveness.

Disciplined application of Lean principles and practices during an economic downturn will prepare the business for when economic conditions improve. However, executives must be vigilant to avoid complacency and backslide into old ways of managing and leading when favorable business conditions return – or when the next downturn comes.

## Notes

[1] "The Toyota Way 2001," Toyota Motor Corporation, internal document, Toyota City, Japan, April 2001

[2] B. Emiliani, *REAL LEAN: The Keys to Sustaining Lean Management*, Volume Three, The CLBM, LLC, Wethersfield, Conn., 2007,

[3] B. Emiliani, *REAL LEAN: Critical Issues and Opportunities in Lean Management*, Volume Two, The CLBM, LLC, Wethersfield, Conn., 2007, Chapters 1-6, 10, and 11

[4] See B. Emiliani, *Practical Lean Leadership: A Strategic Leadership Guide for Executives*, The CLBM, LLC, Wethersfield, Conn., 2008, and B. Emiliani, with D. Stec, L. Grasso, and J. Stodder, *Better Thinking, Better Results: Case Study and Analysis of an Enterprise-Wide Lean Transformation*, second edition, The CLBM, LLC, Wethersfield, Conn., 2007

[5] By "fiscal responsibility" I mean the following: Look at a current state value stream map that depicts conventional batch-and-queue processing of materials and information, full of waste, unevenness, and unreasonableness (managers who do nothing more than manage waste are called "mudanagers"). It is fiscally irresponsible for executives to operate a business in that manner. Compare it with a future state value stream map where material and information flow. That condition depicts fiscal responsibility.

[6] Executives who understand business to be zero-sum (winners and losers), and who therefore lead and manage in zero-sum ways, will not be in compliance with their own corporate ethics policies. Their zero-sum actions will conflict with corporate ethics policies in relation to trust, respect, integrity, fairness, communication, good faith, etc.

[7] See "REVERSE AUCTIONS: A Ten Year Research Project Investigating Business-to-Business Reverse Auctions," M.L. "Bob" Emiliani, http://www.technology.ccsu.edu/personnel/information/emiliani/ra_research.html

[8] B. Emiliani, *REAL LEAN: Critical Issues and Opportunities in Lean Management*, Volume Two, The CLBM, LLC, Wethersfield, Conn., 2007, Chapter 5, "Manage to the Market," pp. 63-73

[9] Flow is how costs and lead times are reduced, how quality is improved, and how customers are satisfied. Flow is the least resource-intensive way to run a business. Flow is healthy for business and for people.

# 3 Learning to Think

*Toyota's management system can rightfully be characterized
as a "Thinking Management System." That puts a special
demand on executives who seek to emulate Toyota's management system: they must learn to think. Being part of a senior
leadership team does not guarantee one's ability to think.
More often it guarantees an inability to think. Recognizing
this will help us understand why so few companies have been
able to practice Lean management with distinction.*

Teruyuki Minoura, the then-president of Toyota Motor
Manufacturing North America, gave a speech in May 2002 in
which he said [1]:

> "When I reflect on what Mr. Ohno taught us, one
> thing that stands out to me is that he taught us how to
> think. He taught us to think deeply. When I think
> about this, I think that perhaps the 'T' in TPS should
> stand not only for Toyota, but also for 'Thinking.'
> The 'Thinking Production System'."

Indeed, Toyota's production system, and in fact their overall
management system, is a "Thinking Management System;" it
requires people to think in ways they have never done before
[2]. People from shop or office floor to the CEO must learn to
think differently all the time. Surprisingly, this is very difficult
for the people at the top of an organization to do, in large part
because they are confident they already know how to think.

Thinking, of course, must be accompanied by *doing*. Sustained efforts must be made to develop the habit of both thinking and doing. Thus, the challenge is to think and do every day, not to solely do things. If people just do things all the time, then they are letting other people think for them. When that happens, they explicitly accept whatever assumptions were used by the thinkers; assumptions which are often incorrect or which have severe limitations. In this way, people fail to learn how to think for themselves.

It is shocking that after decades of effort, the Lean community has few successful Lean leaders in industry that they can point to – meaning, business leaders who put into daily practice both Lean principles: "Continuous Improvement" and "Respect for People." It must be that thinking is really hard to do, and indicates that having confidence in one's ability to think can be a serious misjudgment.

People in industry are often proud to proclaim: "I'm a doer!" The intent, it seems, is to convince others that they have a useful practical orientation; one which will serve their boss's short-term interests. In parallel, the intent is to disparage thinking and people who think, as if thinking always results in pointless theoretical mental exercises that have no home in the workplace.

Thinking requires two human capabilities: intellectualism and rationality. The word "intellectual" has its root in intellect, which in turn relates to intelligence. Thus, intellectualism is the application of intellect; to use one's intelligence. Intellectualism does not hinder leadership capabilities. Nor does it automatically negate one's capabilities to comprehend and act on practical, real-world problems, as many managers seem to believe.

Rationality is the ability to reason methodically and logically, and is a necessary companion to intellectualism.

In general, business leaders have always been anti-intellectual and anti-rational. How can this be? This is not so hard to understand. Intelligence and rational thinking are methodically bred out of people as they rise to the top of organizations, while acceptance of the current state is bred in. What else can explain the dominance of batch-and-queue thinking and practice in modern business since the 1880s? By accepting the current state, managers surrender their capabilities to think and reason logically, especially when it comes to improvement and respecting people.

Most managers who rise through the ranks of organizations have been rewarded for their skills at executing the plan within the framework of established processes – which will almost surely be batch-and-queue – and not for improving plans and processes. After all, that would be seen as taking valuable time and effort away from executing the plan – the doing part of the work, upon which rewards are centered.

We must not forget that mid-level managers and executives typically seek to hire or promote "good soldiers" who will execute the boss's orders without thinking or asking questions [3]. They want people who will "just do it." So in essence, the promotion process in most organizations filters out potential Lean leaders [4]. It's no surprise that there are so few REAL LEAN leaders.

Rising through the ranks in environments that hold "doing" in higher regard than "thinking" – or, better yet, balancing "thinking+doing" – breeds in complacency among executives. This may be hard to imagine, so just look at any current state value stream map depicting batch-and-queue processing, which will likely have existed over generations of managers, and the complacency will be obvious [5].

In Lean management, people are rewarded for executing plans using existing processes, but they are also rewarded for improving plans and processes. It is part of their job requirement to do so, and that is where the iterative, balanced thinking+doing process comes into play. While complacency can be easily bred into people it is impossible to breed out. That is why people at all levels must apply Lean principles and practices every day. Most people, especially executives, severely underestimate the daily practice that is required to become a capable Lean thinker and Lean doer.

Note also that conventional managers do not need to be logical thinkers to execute plans using existing processes. Their business processes, which invariably contain many extra steps and re-work loops, are illogical by definition. These processes embrace waste and high costs as if they are helpful friends. So the underlying design that controls the process, which was worked out by other people long ago, is simply accepted as the best known way to do things. If there were a better way, it would be put into in use, so the (inept) thinking goes. Likewise, managers do not need to be intellectual to execute plans using existing processes.

Scientists and engineers are trained to be intellectual and rational through questioning and the use of the scientific method [6]. To do their job right, they must think and do, but their efforts are often compromised by managers who do things without thinking, often in support (or because) of organizational politics. It is usually clear to most scientists and engineers that organizational politics is anti-intellectual and anti-rational [7]. That is why they often become so utterly frustrated at work and idolize Dilbert® instead of trust their leaders.

As business has become more successful at delivering prosperity, especially to the few at the top, it has become much more influential with respect to its mindset and methods. Current state value stream maps depicting batch-and-queue processing, regardless of the type of business, reflect a deeply embedded brand of anti-intellectualism and anti-rationalism that has steadily gained acceptance, and which has also become more closely aligned with the brand of anti-intellectualism and anti-rationalism that pervades national politics today. As a result, the scientific and engineering brand of intellectualism and rationalism has floundered. However, this is only this brand of intellectualism and rationalism that can move companies forward to the future state.

In order to improve and move forward to the future state, we must recognize anti-intellectualism and anti-rationalism. Here are a few common examples of anti-intellectualism:

- Incurious, and therefore care-free management.
- Repeating the same mistakes.
- Lack of concern for cause-and-effect.
- Saying "there is no free lunch," and then acting in ways where any cost is assumed to be zero.
- Following the herd; e.g. offshoring work.
- Executives who read little or nothing about their cho-

sen profession (i.e. management).

- Preference for information that supports one's view, and ignoring that which does not.

Here are a few common examples of anti-rationalism:

- Keep using metrics that drive wrong behaviors or lead to poor decision-making.
- Managing in ways that marginalize the interests of employees (zero-sum management).
- Squeezing suppliers and thinking they will not try to get even.
- Managing the business as if it serves a sellers' market when it in fact serves buyers' markets.
- Ask employees or customers for their opinions and then ignore them.
- Favoring one function, such as finance, over other functions, such as purchasing.
- Not increasing the wages of workers who have helped improve productivity.

There is no doubt that intellectualism and rationalism can complicate the ways in which we see things. People generally prefer that which is mentally easier to comprehend; it's just human nature to want that.

Despite perhaps some complications, intellectualism and rationalism have the beneficial effect of clarifying things. The fog created by waste-generating organizational politics and self-interest is lifted, which leads to a clearer view of reality that people can then respond to in order to improve. It is not possible to improve if we do not possess an accurate view of reality.

The "Thinking Management System" requires executives to think. If they do think, they will realize that anti-intellectualism and anti-rationalism actually hurt their own efforts and also create negative outcomes for employees, suppliers, customers, communities, and even for investors. That is because problems become systemic and consume ever more resources that could otherwise be shared.

Executives who scorn sharing – and most do – need to think about the efficacy of that position.

**Notes**

[1] T. Minoura, "Address to the World Class Manufacturing Forum," May 2002, http://www.electronics-scotland.com/industry_comment/comment_item.cfm?itemID=18

[2] See T. Ohno, *Toyota Production System*, Productivity Press, Portland, OR, 1988 and S. Hino, *Inside the Mind of Toyota*, Productivity Press, New York, NY, 2006

[3] Doing without thinking means that a lot of costly, stupid things will be done, and repeated. See C. Zimmer, "Children Learn by Monkey See, Monkey Do. Chimps Don't," *The New York Times*, 13 December 2005.

[4] Promotion processes that filter out some of the best and most capable leadership candidates is surely a bad process. Imagine a process that consistently weeded out the best athletes or musicians. Any leader currently in power will no doubt protest and claim they are the best of the best, and steadfastly defend their pay and performance. However, the waste, unevenness, and unreasonableness that exist in business processes and the lack of respect for people indicate that they cannot be the best and that they are grossly overpaid.

[5] M.L. Emiliani and D.J. Stec, "Using Value Stream Maps to Improve Leadership," *Leadership and Organizational Development Journal*, Vol. 25, No. 8, pp. 622-645, 2004

[6] The scientific method "...is a body of techniques for investigating phenomena and acquiring new knowledge, as well as for correcting and integrating previous knowledge. It is based on gathering observable, empirical, [and] measurable evidence, subject to the principles of reasoning" (see http://en.wikipedia.org/wiki/Scientific_method). The four basic steps are: 1) observe a phenomenon; 2) formulate a hypothesis to explain the phenomenon; 3) conduct experiments to prove or disprove hypothesis; and 4) reach a conclusion that validates or modifies the hypothesis.

[7] Many scientists and engineers join the ranks of senior management and begin to exhibit anti-intellectualism and anti-rationalism despite having been trained to be intellectual and rational through questioning and the use of the scientific method. There appears to be a perception, even among scientists and engineers, that the scientific method is less applicable, or not at all applicable, to the duties of managers. This view, of course, is mistaken, but likely is reflected in management courses and leadership training that they have received in school or in professional development training programs. In addition, scientists and engineers who reach the upper echelons of a company will most likely adopt the herd mentality of their peer group which disdains intellectualism and rationalism, and does not think the scientific method can successfully be applied to managerial problems.

# 4 Let's Stop Making the Same Mistake

*Having now recognized the importance of the "Respect for People" principle in Lean management, the Lean community is now more focused than ever on trying to change senior managers' behaviors. However, efforts to change their behaviors in support of new, progressive management practices has, for several decades, largely fallen flat. Knowing this fact should motivate us to re-think the problem and identify processes that are more effective at changing leadership behaviors.*

Wouldn't it be great if top managers could easily see the wide-ranging benefits of Lean management and the vast array of improvements and human and organizational capability-building that are possible? If they could see it, then you would think that they would rush to change their leadership behaviors in order to secure the gains for the business and its stakeholders as soon as possible. But as we all know, this rarely happens. The usual outcome is for executives to take the business down the Lean path with little or no change in their leadership behaviors.

Trainers, consultants, and other interested parties focus their efforts on trying to change leadership behaviors because such changes are essential to correctly practice Lean management. However, their record of success is poor. Changing the leadership behaviors of successful people with big egos is a quest whose probability for success is very low. You can be sure there have been and will continue to be a few isolated examples of leaders who have successfully changed some of their behaviors, but there will not be much more than that.

It is erroneous to think that the answer lies in changing executives' leadership behaviors. This critical error has been made repeatedly in the past [1] with the antecedent to Lean management, Scientific Management [2, 3] in the early 1900s, again in the last 35 years with Lean, and also with the scores of narrowly-focused management fads that have come and gone over the years.

I have been hot on the trail of leadership behaviors as the key to Lean success since the 1995. I even wrote one half-dozen scholarly (yet always practical) papers that made important new contributions to our understanding of Lean leadership behaviors. However, it turns out that I made the same mistake that so many people made before me, and that leaders of the Lean management movement are again making today.

I realized in 2002 why we were on the wrong track. It was because the way the problem had been conceptualized was too narrow. The long-term consensus view among human resource professionals, industrial psychologists, organizational behavior specialists, and leadership experts is that changes in behaviors will lead to the desired new leadership competencies. Thus:

Behavior ⟶ Competency

The fatal flaw here is that it ignores executives' beliefs about business, markets, economics, employees, customers, suppliers, investors, quality, information, know-how, etc. It assumes that all executives share the same beliefs, which they do not. Executives who go though competency model based leadership training will learn some useful things, but it is mostly back to business – and back to behaviors and competencies – as usual a few weeks after the training ends. It is not surprising that traditional leadership competency models do not work so well.

That is why I have, for the last several years, de-emphasized the behavioral aspects of my Lean leadership training. Instead, I place much more emphasis on the antecedent to executive behaviors – their beliefs, and also the major and minor inter-relationships between beliefs, behaviors, and competencies. This approach has proven to be far more enlightening and useful to executives.

The beliefs that executives have are non-uniform. For example, most executives manage in a zero-sum fashion (winners and losers) while some manage in a non-zero-sum fashion (win-win). We know this empirically by observing executives who practice conventional management (zero-sum) and those who are skilled at practicing REAL LEAN management (non-zero-sum) [4]. As a result, the framework for understanding the problem must be revised as follows:

$$\text{Belief} \longrightarrow \text{Behavior} \longrightarrow \text{Competency}$$

Beliefs are important because they are the foundation upon which leaders reason and evaluate competing courses of action; they are the basis for executive decision-making processes. If an executive believes that business is a zero-sum activity, then the "Respect for People" principle will never be understood or practiced no matter how much an executive coach or trainer, or the executive, tries to change behaviors to yield Lean leader competencies.

The "Respect for People" principle in Lean management requires leaders to first change their beliefs that business can be successful as a non-zero-sum endeavor, which will then support new Lean behaviors, and, in turn, lead to new Lean leadership competencies. Experience has shown that this is nearly impossible to do using the thinking and training methods rooted in organizational behavior and leadership development disciplines.

Let me give you a concrete example. The transfer and exchange of knowledge and information horizontally across a company so that people can improve is called "yokoten" by Toyota people. Senior managers must practice the "Respect for People" in order for yokoten to occur. Sharing knowledge and information will be minimal if employees fear for their jobs, such as when management views Lean as nothing more than zero-sum cost-cutting, resulting in layoffs. Employees suffering under management's practice of "Fake Lean" (meaning only the "Continuous Improvement" principle is practiced) will instead hoard knowledge and information to reduce risk and to survive.

Most executives prefer the "my way or the highway," zero-sum approach to leadership and the execution of strategy and day-to-day tasks, in part because it seems much easier to lead that way. But this reveals intellectual weakness, or at least a systematic disdain for knowledge and information, as well as intolerance for ambiguity, which creates and sustains the psychological necessity for authoritarian rule. As should be expected, horizontal knowledge and information transfer is not relevant in organizations led by autocratic, zero-sum-minded executives. Behavioral change programs for executives who lead this way will be mostly unsuccessful.

Despite this, we keep making the same mistake when we think that new behaviors will lead to new Lean competencies – without needing to address the boss' underlying beliefs. The question then, is: How do you get executives to change their beliefs? This sounds like an impossible task, but it is not.

Experience, again, has shown that the most effective process is kaizen. By kaizen I mean where problems are quickly studied and changes are made immediately to eliminate waste, unevenness, and unreasonableness, and where the three principles of kaizen are in always use: process and results, systems focus, and non-blaming, non-judgmental. I do not mean the degenerate form of (fake) kaizen that has become common in recent years in which people plan what changes to make and then seek management's permission to make the proposed changes, and where the three principles of kaizen are not practiced.

The challenge, of course, is to get executives to regularly participate in kaizen [5-8]. Most executives will not participate in kaizen because they fear looking stupid, losing status or control, or don't think they have anything to learn. The problem is that *seeing* waste, unevenness, and unreasonableness, first-hand, is *believing*. By not participating in kaizen, executives forego the opportunity to see new things and believe in new things.

Most executives are extraordinarily loyal to conventional management in part because it has served them very well, and also because of the huge sunk cost associated with decades-long personal efforts to become skilled at leading a business filled with waste, unevenness, and unreasonableness. So they find many reasons to avoid participating in kaizen, such as claiming they are too busy, and delegate that activity to employees at lower levels.

However, lower-level employees participating in properly facilitated kaizens develop new beliefs while the executives do not. This soon becomes immensely frustrating for them because their beliefs start to diverge from those of the senior leadership team which soon leads to enormous communication and knowledge gaps. Eventually, lower-level people lose interest in participating in kaizen because it is too difficult to get senior managers to understand what they have seen first-hand and what they now believe. So they simply give up.

Daily kaizen [9] is an absolute requirement for executives who wish to learn and practice REAL LEAN management, and who wish for employees at all levels of the organization to develop proficiency in the proper application of Lean principles and practices. The problem is that kaizen humbles people who do not want to be humbled.

Kaizen at work is like golf at play. The game of golf quickly teaches its players that they are not perfect; they are humbled many times in each round of golf (if not each hole) by the mistakes they make.

Kaizen is not a game, but, like golf, every kaizen quickly teaches executives that they are not perfect, they make many mistakes, and that they are not as smart as they think they are. It seems that many executives can easily handle humbling experiences outdoors, but have great difficulty dealing with humbling experiences indoors.

Daily participation in kaizen by executives is a simple and effective countermeasure to the long-standing problem of how to get leaders to change their behaviors. It begins with changing beliefs, and kaizen is more effective than anything else in doing that. So don't waste time or money doing other things. Just accept kaizen as the necessary and most effective process.

A few years ago I wrote a couple of practical papers that made important new contributions to our understanding of Lean leadership beliefs and the role of kaizen. They are titled: "Linking Leaders' Beliefs to their Behaviors and Competencies" (published in 2003) and "Using Value Stream Maps to Improve Leadership" (published in 2004). You can read them at www.theclbm.com/publications.

They show the dramatic difference between the beliefs, behaviors, and competencies of leaders skilled in wasteful conventional management compared to Lean leaders. You will be amazed how simple current state value stream maps can also be used to diagnose and correct seemingly intractable leadership problems. And you will see why kaizen is the key.

I hope you will take advantage of these innovative and practical works so that we can stop making the same mistake.

**Notes**

[1] B. Emiliani, *REAL LEAN: Critical Issues and Opportunities in Lean Management*, Volume Two, The CLBM, LLC, Wethersfield, Conn., 2007, Chapter 1-6 and 10

[2] F.W. Taylor, *The Principles of Scientific Management*, Harper & Brothers Publishers, New York, NY, 1911

[3] W. Tsutsui, *Manufacturing Ideology: Scientific Management in Twentieth-Century Japan*, Princeton University Press, Princeton New Jersey, 1998

[4] B. Emiliani, *Practical Lean Leadership: A Strategic Leadership Guide for Executives*, The CLBM, LLC, Wethersfield, Conn., 2008

[5] M. Imai, *Kaizen*, McGraw-Hill, New York, NY, 1986 and M. Imai, *Gemba Kaizen*, McGraw-Hill, New York, NY, 1997

[6] "The Toyota Way 2001," Toyota Motor Corporation, internal document, Toyota City, Japan, April 2001

[7] B. Emiliani, with D. Stec, L. Grasso, and J. Stodder, *Better Thinking, Better Results: Case Study and Analysis of an Enterprise-Wide Lean Transformation*, second edition, The CLBM, LLC, Wethersfield, Conn., 2007

[8] J. Liker and M. Hoseus, *Toyota Culture*, McGraw-Hill, New York, NY, 2008

[9] Daily participation in kaizen among executives can occur through many means, ranging from the application of Lean principles and practices to their own daily work activities, to 2-hour kaizens, half-day kaizens, kaizens 3-5 days in duration, etc. The point is to apply Lean principles and practices in a consistent manner every day on an individual basis and also periodically on a team basis.

# 5 Don't Aim Low

*For decades people have used the term "Lean manufactur-ing." In recent years people have started using the term "operational excellence." Continuing to view Lean management narrowly as an operating practice leads to many unfavorable consequences.*

What's in a name? It may not seem like much, but how we refer to things makes a big difference in how people perceive them. For decades people used the term "Lean manufacturing" or "Lean production" [1]. The obvious implication is that Lean is a "manufacturing thing," and therefore not applicable to anyone in any department outside of manufacturing. As a result we have experienced decades of delay in the application of Lean principles and practices in other parts of the company.

Likewise, service business executives saw the term "Lean manufacturing" and steered clear of Lean because their com-panies did not manufacture anything. Again, we experienced decades of delay in the application on Lean principle and practices in service organizations.

These delays and misapplication of Lean principles and prac-tices are not beneficial to the spread of Lean management. Their likely effect is to deepen negative perceptions of Lean management among those most in need of change. So the name we use is important, but it is certainly not the only thing that matters.

The term "Lean manufacturing" is finally losing its luster.

The correct term is "Lean management," but we're not yet there in terms of its widespread use. Now we have the term "operational excellence" (previously, "manufacturing excellence") to describe both the intent and outcome of Lean management. Stubbornly sticking to the narrow view that Lean is nothing more than an operating practice has at least four significant unfavorable consequences:

1. Perpetuates inaccurate views
Most top executives view operations as a dirty, inferior activity (compared to finance or sales, for example) that consists of simple repetitive tasks. Why are they unable to see that activities in every other department, as well as their own activities, are also mostly repetitive tasks? Why do senior managers assume that operations needs to be excellent, but other departments don't, or, that they are already excellent? Why not "Marketing Excellence," "Financial Excellence," "Engineering Excellence," etc? In most companies, these departments are far from excellent.

2. Reduces speed
Most executives share the same regret in hindsight of some important activity: not moving faster. So why would they slow down their Lean transformation by misunderstanding it as operational excellence? Why would they want to make only operations more competitive and maintain the status-quo in all other departments? Managers must work to improve company competitiveness, not just the competitiveness of operations.

3. Undercuts teamwork
Most executives endlessly exhort employees on the need for

teamwork. So why would they undercut teamwork by applying Lean principles and practices only in operations? Why is the operations team doing things that the finance or engineering team isn't? Why be exclusive when you can, and should, be inclusive?

4. Limits learning
Most executives talk about how employees must commit to lifelong learning. So why would they offer that opportunity to people in operations and not to people in other departments? Why do senior managers assume that operations people have much to learn, but others do not? Doesn't learning via the application continuous improvement tools and processes apply to everyone, including senior managers?

In addition, "operational excellence" will take a company only so far. It leads to a false sense of security. A company has to be good at doing many other things such as new product development, marketing, sales, etc. The business landscape is littered with thousands of companies that had excellent operations, only to suffer serious financial distress because they failed to recognize or respond to changes in customer wants and needs [2].

When CEOs aim for "operational excellence," they are aiming low. The pressure for improvement is surely on the vice president of operations, but the other executives are largely off the hook. They can more-or-less keep doing what they have always done. In addition to being short-sighted, it is not fair to the people in operations and thus is inconsistent with the "Respect for People" principle.

Senior managers cannot learn the craft of Lean management by focusing their efforts solely on operations. While there is much to learn in operations – not the least of which is to recognize operations as the central value-creating activity [3], not an inferior activity – there is as much to learn in every other part of the company, including shipping and receiving.

Imagine you are a carpenter. You cannot become a woodworking craftsman by making only coffee tables. You must also learn to make chairs, dressers, cabinets, know how to frame a house, etc. You must know how to apply your knowledge of carpentry principles and practices to different types of work.

Similarly, you can not learn the craft of Lean management by applying Lean principles and practices only in operations. Managers must have cross-functional experiences in three or four different parts of the company – operations, sales, finance, information systems, purchasing, R&D, etc. – and have participated in the application of Lean principles and practices in each functional area they work in, and then apply them to different types of work.

That's how you learn the craft of Lean management.

**Notes**

[1] J. Womack, D. Jones, and D. Roos, *The Machine That Changed the World*, Rawson Associates, New York, NY, 1990

[2] Achieving "operational excellence" is no guarantee of future success. Indeed, many companies have achieved "operational excellence" at some point in their history, such as: Ford Motor Company in the 1910s-1920s; Morris Motors (UK) in the 1920s-1930s; Dell Computer in the 1990s; or Delphi Corporation in the 1990s. Operational excellence turned out to be short-lived. What they instead found was that inattentiveness to end-use customers' wants and needs created crippling financial problems. It necessary to be Lean in operations, but it is not sufficient. The entire enterprise must apply Lean principles and practices.

[3] Operations is the principal cash-generating activity in manufacturing and service businesses, and thus should be of great interest to the entire senior management team.

# 6 The Eighth Waste

*Taiichi Ohno and his colleagues identified seven wastes in business processes. But is there an eighth waste? Is there a ninth waste? A tenth waste? There is definitely an eighth waste; a waste that is specific to the process of human interaction. It is fitting that there should be a waste specific to human interaction between stakeholders – especially managers and workers – because business cannot exist without people.*

In 1998 after several years of Lean implementation experience in the manufacturing shop and supply chain, I wrote a paper titled "Lean Behaviors" [1]. In that paper I formally identified, defined, and characterized what I saw as the eighth waste, a waste that Ohno and his colleagues had not specifically identified. However, an unnamed waste was repeatedly referred to in the writings of Ohno and other retired Toyota executives [2, 3]. Both relate to leadership behaviors.

I named the eighth waste "behavioral waste," and defined it as:

> Behaviors that consume resources but create
> no value for customers.

The context for the eighth waste is the leadership behaviors of senior managers, not the behaviors of shop floor or office personnel. The reason why is because people at lower levels mirror the behaviors of those above them. It is the responsibility of senior leaders to exhibit the behaviors that they expect to see from lower-level people. Unfortunately, this is often not the case.

Leaders, sometimes unknowingly, behave in dysfunctional, wasteful ways, especially in conventionally managed business where the concept of "waste" is unknown [4]. These wasteful behaviors signal to subordinates that it is OK to behave the same way, and many do just that because they can see that it results in certain advantages such as professional advancement.

While we like to think that promotions are based mostly on merit, the reality is they are often based more on social and political considerations. There is a strong tendency for bosses to promote people who are good at mirroring their behaviors – especially their bad behaviors [5] – because, like the boss, they are perceived as tough, loyal, and dedicated.

The problem is that this perpetuates a sense among employees that nothing much ever changes. The boss's bad behaviors and the non-merit based criteria upon which many people are promoted are obviously antithetical to both the "Continuous Improvement" and "Respect for People" principles.

Many Lean practitioners today know intuitively that there has to be an eighth waste, and that it is related to people because people are critical actors in the process of getting things done in the workplace. There seems to be something that is obviously missing in Ohno's seven waste construct, so they identify one or more of the following as the eighth waste:

- Waste of creativity
- Waste of intellect
- Waste of human potential
- Wasted ideas
- Underutilized minds
- Underutilized people

The context for these typically, but not exclusively, relate to people at lower levels in an organization; the people who do the value-creating work that end-use customers pay for. It is their creativity that is wasted, for example. It does not refer to managers, who are seen as the principal actors that create the eighth waste.

If you think about each one of these deeply, you will recognize them as symptoms of one or more problems. That would lead you to do simple root cause analyses to understand the true cause of the problem. For example, you would ask:

1. Why are people underutilized?
   - *Managers do not know how to utilize people.*
2. Why don't managers know how to utilize people?
   - *They don't know what people are capable of.*
3. Why don't managers know what people are capable of?
   - *They don't find out what they can do.*
4. Why don't managers find out what people can do?
   - *They don't think they need to know.*
5. Why do managers think they do not need to know?
   - *They think they already know what people can do.*
6. Why do managers think they already know what people can do?
   - *They are overconfident in their knowledge of what people can do.*
7. Why are managers overconfident in their knowledge of what people can do?
   - *Most managers have big egos.*
8. Why do most managers have big egos?
   - *They have not received negative feedback.*
9. Why haven't managers received negative feedback?

> - *People are afraid to give negative feedback.*
> 10. Why are people afraid to give negative feedback?
> - *They fear consequences that could be harmful to their career.*

There are two interesting parts of this 5 Whys analysis. The first relates to manager's ego (Why #7). Having an ego is certainly no problem. But having an oversized ego is a really big problem. It typically leads to an assumption that one knows it all, at least when it comes to mundane things such as knowing what people are capable of. Bosses with big egos are certain to behave in wasteful ways. The second is fear (Why #10). People who fear their boss usually avoid giving feedback and are clearly responding to his or her wasteful behaviors.

So it turns out that the bad behaviors exhibited by senior leaders is indeed the eighth waste. However, if you dig even deeper you will find that behavioral waste is caused by other things [6]. For now we'll stay focused on leaders' behavioral waste.

Most Lean practitioners think that leaders' behaviors cannot be measured, are not actionable, and that it is very difficult to identify practical countermeasures. This is not the case. Behavioral waste is measurable and actionable, and practical countermeasures can be easily identified, as we showed in our groundbreaking paper titled: "Using Value Stream Maps to Improve Leadership" [6].

Senior managers must recognize the existence of the eighth waste because: 1) it is real, and 2) it enables them to comprehend and put into practice the "Respect for People" principle [3, 7]. Most senior managers are unaware of behavioral waste, so it is no surprise that we rarely see them practicing the "Respect for People" principle. Instead, they focus on continuous improvement, invariably with only limited success.

It is worth noting that the leaders of progressive industrial management practice since the 1890s have consistently recognized that wasteful leadership behaviors weaken the practice of continuous improvement [8]. The inability of executives to recognize and comprehend the eighth waste impedes a company's Lean efforts and the Lean movement in general. It also leads to intense criticisms of Lean management that diminish its relevance over time.

Almost all of the Lean training that has been fielded over the last 30 years has ignored the existence of behavioral waste. The narrow focus on applying Lean tools and processes to the shop floor to achieve short-term gains has done great harm. Lean training has also consistently ignored the "Respect for People" principle.

In general, the trainers succumb to faulty assumptions that behavioral waste and the "Respect for People" principle are:

- Not measurable
- Not actionable
- Too difficult a topic to present to executives
- Will provoke negative reactions
- Will insult executives' intelligence
- Things that executives already do

So Lean trainers, if they do anything, approach behavioral waste and the "Respect for People" principle using the same type of basic soft skills training that you would find in any conventional leadership development course. In other words, they do not directly address behavioral waste and the "Respect for People" principle; they skip over it. This approach is flawed and inadequate.

Ignoring behavioral waste and the "Respect for People" principle sets the trainers and the trainees (the executives) up to fail. Both must be a part of Lean training along with many specific, practical examples. The key takeaway for trainees is that the "Respect for People" principle must be part of their daily practice. Ignoring the "Respect for People" principle is the dominant failure mode in Lean transformations. That being the case, both trainers and executives should make careful preparations to avoid this failure mode.

Some executives will remain unconvinced that behavioral waste is a big problem, or that each member of the leadership team must practice the "Respect for People" principle daily. The hold-outs should find the following to be convincing.

Most executives believe in the basic tenets of Adam Smith's classical economics [9] (which they should question, of course [10, 11]):

- People are rational self-interested maximizers.
- The "invisible hand" guides people towards this end, which results in greater good to society.
- Taxes are a necessary evil (to pay for roads, for example), but which cause distortions and reduce economic efficiency.
- Regulation is bad because it reduces economic efficiency.

If you believe that, then you will have no problem believing that behavioral waste, the driver of destructive organizational politics, exists, is bad, and that you can do something to reduce or eliminate it. Let's look more closely at taxes and regulation.

Behavioral waste also functions as a tax on organizations which causes distortions that reduce corporate operating (and non-operating) efficiency – particularly the interactions between human beings who are the enablers (or blockers) of material and information flows. In essence, executives self-impose large taxes (behavioral waste) and crippling regulations (organizational politics) upon themselves and the company. The economic efficiency of organizations is reduced by behavioral waste, organizational politics, and zero-sum practices. That does not sound like what rational self-interested maximizers would do. The obvious lesson is that the "invisible hand" makes mistakes and can be a poor guide at times.

Executives who have the attitude that organizational politics and behavioral waste are a fact of life set the bar very low for themselves and their direct reports. In doing so they reveal their unhealthy and illogical willingness to live with mountains of behavioral waste. Instead of fomenting organizational politics and tolerating widespread behavioral waste, top management should seek to reduce and even eliminate it [12].

Executives, economists, finance people, and many others have long been fond of saying: "There ain't no such thing as a free lunch." But that cannot be true. They obviously think there is a free lunch when it comes to organizational politics and behavioral waste. They think these are free; that they result in no costs to an organization or its stakeholders (e.g.

suppliers or investors). They are wrong; the costs are great. Simple spreadsheets can be created to show this [13], though it is not at all necessary to do so. You can clearly see the costs are great simply by comparing current state value stream maps, which are high in organizational politics and behavioral waste, to future state value stream maps, which are low in organizational politics and behavioral waste [6].

Executives would do well to understand that behavioral waste is not an ethereal mist that quickly evaporates. Instead it is a thick, choking cloud that lingers and undergoes a transformation in properties from human behaviors to tangible business metrics, including:

- Time; as in the time it takes people to do something
- Quantity; the number of items completed
- Quality; defects and re-work
- Economic variables; processing costs, profits and loss, etc.
- Semi-quantitative data; employee survey results

It is analogous to the Fourier transform in mathematics [14] in which one function (time) is transformed into another (frequency). In our case, wasteful leadership behaviors are transformed into real business problems represented by familiar business metrics such as time (slower), quantity (fewer), quality (lower), cost (higher), etc.

$$\mathcal{F}$$
$$f(l_b) \iff F(t, q_1, q_2\, c, s, \ldots)$$

The effect of leaders' behavioral waste on other people, and also on process and purpose, is dramatic and consequential, though the cause may seem trifling from executives' perspective. These human behaviors are transformed into other properties that create innumerable business problems, which add cost but do not create value for end-use customers.

Learning the craft of Lean management requires executives to recognize and respond to things that they have previously ignored, thereby becoming more highly skilled. It is similar to vintners who can discern the most subtle differences between fine cabernet sauvignons. Or luthiers who can hear the difference in tone between different types of woods, small changes in the thickness of the top, or the location of the soundboard. Or visual artists who see light, color, form, and texture in extremely nuanced ways.

Craftsmen recognize subtleties that amateurs cannot. Small things loom big to the craftsman, and what the amateur sees as big are small. In conventional management, behavioral waste is not perceived as anything more than a trifling annoyance that can be fixed simply by developing a thicker skin. In Lean management, behavioral waste is perceived as a huge problem that must be corrected because it impedes flow. In conventional management, respecting people is not valued and basically left to the discretion of individual managers. In Lean management, all managers must practice the "Respect for People" principle.

In Fake Lean management, workers own the seven wastes: overproduction, waiting, transportation, processing itself (not over-processing), inventory, movement, and defects. In REAL LEAN, management owns all eight wastes. Executives have a special, personal responsibility to eliminate the eighth waste [12]. Doing so is completely consistent with their fiduciary responsibilities to shareholders [15] and their responsibilities to other stakeholders.

In his book *Toyota Production System*, Taiichi Ohno said [16]:

> "The greatest waste of all is excess inventory."

This is certainly true with respect to waste in processes used to create goods or services. However, the *worst* waste of all is the eighth waste, behavioral waste, because it degrades the human experience.

Executives who exhibit behavioral waste weaken employees, as well as other key stakeholders (such as suppliers). Intentionally or not, their behavioral waste diminishes human creativity, spirit, energy, motivation, commitment, optimism, courage, teamwork, fair dealing, diversity, and trust.

That's no way to lead a business [17].

**Notes**

[1] M.L. Emiliani, "Lean Behaviors," *Management Decision*, Vol. 36, No. 9, pp. 615-631, 1998

[2] T. Ohno, *Toyota Production System*, Productivity Press, Portland, OR, 1988, pp. 19-20

[3] B. Emiliani, *REAL LEAN: The Keys to Sustaining Lean Management*, Volume Three, The CLBM, LLC, Wethersfield, Conn., 2008, Appendix I, "The Equally Important 'Respect for People' Principle," pp. 121-137

[4] In a conventionally managed business, the term "waste" is used casually, such as: "That's a waste of time," or, "We wasted money on that project." It is not defined rigorously as it is in Lean management, as: activities that consume resources but create no value for end-use customers.

[5] Based on my research, over 80 percent of supervisors possess numerous wasteful behavioral that result in poor relationships with subordinates (some 75 percent of workers who switch jobs do so because of relationship problems with their supervisors). This implies that the long-wave trend has been to promote people who mirror their boss's behaviors, which are similarly wasteful, and illustrates the extent to which behavioral waste goes unrecognized and uncorrected. Will you commit to reversing this trend?

[6] M.L. Emiliani and D.J. Stec, "Using Value Stream Maps to Improve Leadership," *Leadership and Organizational Development Journal*, Vol. 25, No. 8, pp. 622-645, 2004

[7] "The Toyota Way 2001," Toyota Motor Corporation, internal document, Toyota City, Japan, April 2001

[8] B. Emiliani, *REAL LEAN: Critical Issues and Opportunities in Lean Management*, Volume Two, The CLBM, LLC, Wethersfield, Conn., 2007, Chapters 1-6, 10, and 11

[9] A. Smith, *The Wealth of Nations*, 1776; Bantam Classics Reprint Edition, 2003

[10] See B. Emiliani, *REAL LEAN: The Keys to Sustaining Lean Management*, Volume Three, The CLBM, LLC, Wethersfield, Conn., 2008. A note on "The Wealth of Corporations:" In general, people tend to buy expensive cars, houses, and other goods and services that are far in excess of their actual needs. Those who do this could rightly be characterized as impractical and wasteful. Could being impractical and wasteful in one's personal life carry over to business life? Maybe so. I would bet that not one senior manager of a Fortune® 500 corporation would characterize themselves as impractical and wasteful at work. Instead, they would say that they watch the bottom line very closely, make prudent decisions, and only

do the things that matter most for real people such as shareholders. However, nearly every senior management team runs the business using conventional (batch-and-queue, zero-sum) management practices which are rife with impracticality and waste. Surprisingly, most executives do not see the impracticality and waste. Conventional management therefore represents opulence. It is a luxury management practice whose cost is far greater than that actually needed by the business to deliver the value that its customers seek. This luxurious management practice voraciously consumes all resources – time, money, materials, human energy and spirit, etc. – and reflects a steadfast mindset among senior managers that the company is wealthy enough to afford the high cost of conventional management. No company is that wealthy. Similarly, no nation is wealthy enough to afford the high cost of conventional management.

[11] Proponents of Adam Smith's work must be careful to distinguish between the absolute and the conditional in classical economics. That which may seem to be a universal truth could be grounded in flawed logic, thus narrowing its scope of applicability or rendering it impractical (see J.K. Ingram, *A History of Political Economy*, Macmillan and Co., New York, NY, 1888, pp. 240-246). Dedicated Lean thinkers seek to avoid dogma and mental rigidity because it can obscure reality. A clear view of reality is prized by Lean leaders because it enables them to do important things that leaders of conventionally managed business cannot do or have great difficulty doing, such as: applying the "Respect for People" principle, quickly responding to changing market conditions, getting the facts, making accurate decisions, teamwork, organically growing the business, working collaboratively with suppliers, growing market share, increasing profitability, etc.

[12] B. Emiliani, *Practical Lean Leadership: A Strategic Leadership Guide for Executives*, The CLBM, LLC, Wethersfield, Conn., 2008

[13] B. Maskell and B. Baggaley, *Practical Lean Accounting*, Productivity Press, New York, NY, 2004

[14] See http://en.wikipedia.org/wiki/Fourier_transform

[15] Eliminating the eighth waste is also consistent with executives' ethical responsibilities.

[16] T. Ohno, *Toyota Production System*, Productivity Press, Portland, OR, 1988, p. 54

[17] Behavioral waste has many unfavorable effects on a business. One is productivity, which is so important to corporate and national wealth creation. Executives have long focused on increasing productivity by driving

process improvements and investing in new technology. It would be wise to expand upon the means for improving productivity by adding a third approach: the elimination of behavioral waste in the leadership team. If executives are serious about this, then they will have to acknowledge the unpleasant fact that there is a much higher proportion of sub-criminal psychopaths in the executive ranks (some 55 percent or more of managers are psychopaths [synonymous with the term sociopaths]) than in the general population (~1 percent). This should not be surprising; the starting point for corporate psychopathic behaviors among managers can be as simple as believing in the saying: "business is business" – when, in fact, business is human. Performance appraisal data or feedback from subordinates will lead you to find executives who are candidates for developing Lean behaviors. If, after three or four rounds of corrective action, the executive still exhibits significant behavioral waste, then it is probably time to part ways. They won't like the company anyway and will likely welcome the opportunity to work elsewhere (the competition?), where they can better utilize their "strengths."

# 7 The Other Information System

*Say the words "information system" and computer hardware and software always comes to mind. But every company actually has two information systems. One is machine (computer hardware and software), and the other is human – the people who work in the company. The human information system is often neglected but must be managed much more carefully than the machine information system.*

Humans have had a fascination with machines since ancient times. The drive to implement new, higher technology machines in business is ever-present as managers seek to gain competitive advantage. In general, new industrial machinery has been very beneficial. It has steadily relieved workers of dangerous and physically-demanding work, improved productivity, and provided opportunities to learn new skills and apply more brainpower to the job.

Often, however, investment in new machinery turns out to have harsh unintended consequences because managers consistently overestimate what machines can do. Examples of expensive mistakes abound, and people generally have great difficulty applying lessons-learned to avoid repeating the same mistakes. Another common problem is confusing the relationship between machines and people. Should people serve machines or should machines serve people?

Over the last 50 years, computer hardware and software have taken on increasing importance in post-modern business processes. Unfortunately, in most cases people serve the machine when the machine should serve the people. The former is common today, particularly with respect to expensive enterprise software systems.

Every company has two information systems: One is computer hardware and software, and the other is the people who work in the company [1]. In the case of computer hardware and software, many different types of information technology specialists are employed to design, manage, and service the information system infrastructure. Company executives play various roles in supporting their efforts to manage information using machines.

But what is the role of the executive team when it comes to managing the human information system? Is it their responsibility to facilitate information flows between people? If so, how should they do that? Should they seek to retain human information long-term, or should they freely let it go?

Senior managers are the leaders of an organization. What they do as leaders is normally described in terms of generalized skills and personality characteristics, which are inputs. However, let's describe leadership differently in terms of outputs: information flow [2]. That is, a key role of leadership is to be enablers of human information system flow, and not to constrict, distort, or block information flows.

Describing leadership in terms of information flow re-contextualizes leadership; how they must think, how they must behave, and what they must know and do. This will help clarify their role and provide clearer direction and specific, practical actions they must take. This proves to be much easier to do than trying to emulate hard-to-define personality characteristics such as charisma.

Executives have two roles with respect to the human information system. They are both information system administrators and software engineers. In either role they can do things that facilitate information flow – which is what they should be doing – or they can make it difficult, or nearly impossible for information to flow. Why would executives make it difficult or nearly impossible for information to flow? Often it is for selfish reasons, such as to preserve self-image or self-interest.

Recall that the previous chapter described the *worst* waste of all: the eighth waste, behavioral waste. Executives can knowingly or unknowingly disrupt information flows to achieve local, department-level objectives. Or, they could disrupt information flows simply because they accept the existence of behavioral waste and assume nothing can be done to eliminate it. In both cases, they are introducing malicious software (*malware*) into the human information system, which disrupts information flows and leads to many recurring errors.

How do executives do this? One way is to introduce a *virus*, which is a leadership behavior that can copy itself and infect other persons without their knowledge. Examples of viruses that infect human information systems include: distrust, blame, arrogance, selfishness, and bullying. Leaders who exhibit these behaviors, which create no value for any customer, corrupt or modify other people's behaviors. They become like their boss, warts and all.

Executives can also introduce a *worm* into the organization, which is a self-replicating behavior that is copied onto other departments (nodes). An example of a particularly disruptive worm is organizational politics, which consumes huge amounts of bandwidth – that is, the throughput of information across the network. Organizational politics shifts people's attention from their customers and focuses them on their own small internal company world. Another example is the biases and stereotypes that executives exhibit with respect to certain departments. For example, top executives often favor certain departments, such as finance, strategic planning, or sales and marketing, over others, such as operations, purchasing, or human resources [3].

What other types of malicious behaviors (code) could the leaders of a company introduce? They could introduce *Trojan horses*, which is when leaders appear to do one thing but instead do another. An example of this is when the boss sends someone to become part of a team, but instructs that person to make sure the department's interests are not threatened or kill certain ideas. Another Trojan horse is when senior managers ask for workers' input but ignore it, and, instead, do what they planned to do all along or give preference to the advice of outsiders.

Executives can also introduce *spyware*, which is when leaders seek to surreptitiously monitor someone's interaction with others. An example of this is when the boss asks someone to do one thing, and then instructs a different person to monitor what is happening and intervene to achieve a different, often pre-determined outcome. Siloed organizations tend to launch lots of spyware and exhibit unilateralist tendencies instead of teamwork.

Executives are famous for sending out *spam*, which are unsolicited verbal, written, or video messages that attempt to sell people on certain ideas or actions. A prime example of this is corporate communications, especially slogans, which employees generally recognize as empty because the bosses fail to walk their talk.

Senior managers can also fall prey to *bugs* in the human information system, which are flaws that prevent the system from functioning as intended. Examples of this include bad ideas and shortcuts, which are used liberally by executives [4]. Other types of bugs, such as sticking to the plan despite the existence of new information or the inability to admit mistakes, can cause the system to crash.

Viruses, worms, Trojan horses, spyware, and spam are common in most organizations. This means that senior managers often fail in their efforts to manage the human information system; to enable accurate and high-quality information flows that are widely available on-demand. Imagine computer information system administrators or software engineers who regularly introduced viruses, worms, Trojan horses, spyware, and spam. They would be seen as worse than incompetent and immediately lose their job.

These threats to the human information system are not free. They have large costs that require extensive resources to fix. The normal route taken by senior managers is to simply guess at what caused the problem [5] and then hire a consultant to deliver a training program (a *patch*) to the workforce. Machines, the computer hardware and software, are easy to fix. The problems caused by poor design and systemic mismanagement of the human information system are more challenging.

A company and its capabilities are comprised of both a human information system as well as a computer information system. Both have important roles to play in executing the value-creating activities that end-use customers are willing to pay for.

In order to prosper long-term, a company must grow. To do that, the company – its people – must add new information to both the human and the computer information systems. The ability to do so successfully results in enterprise-wide capability-building [6], which leads to strong organic growth. That's what you truly want.

The inability to add new information to both the human and the computer information systems results in a loss of capabilities. Senior managers often intentionally discard human information and corporate capabilities in their efforts to cut costs; for example, by sending work to low-wage countries or selling assets. They willingly give away valuable information and corporate capabilities to other companies and layoff the employees who had the knowledge needed to satisfy customers.

Trashing the human information system means that capabilities are lost, which then makes it much more difficult to grow organically. This frustrates senior managers and soon propels them to adopt alternate strategies to grow, all of which are expensive, complex, risky, and ultimately offer relief for only a short period of time. They will typically try to grow through forced means such as mergers, acquisitions, divestitures, etc.

[7], or game the financial metrics [8].

The leaders' role is to get information to flow between humans, not to introduce malware (behavioral waste) that constricts, distorts, or blocks the flow of information, or causes the human information system to crash. Lots of malware in the human information system is like having numerous unwanted computer programs that run the background on your computer. They consume the organization's random access memory (RAM) – the pre-frontal cortex computing area of the human brain. It also makes it difficult build capabilities and write important new information onto an organizations' hard drive – the part of the human brain called the basal ganglia. This is why mangers think workers are the problem and why workers think managers are the problem.

Managers are fond of machines because, unlike humans, they don't get pissed-off and withhold information. However, while they do not withhold information, it is a mistake to think that the information contained in machines is always accurate or relevant. Business is human [9] and business needs humans; it needs employees to create and deliver products and services. It is not wise to think that business can be run without them, or that executives can freely introduce malware and that doing so has zero costs.

There is no doubt that it is a great challenge to manage today's machine-based information systems, and that executives have important roles to play in their management. However, the human information system is as valuable, if not more valuable, because it contains both tacit knowledge and explicit knowledge [10]. Therefore, executives must manage the human information system more carefully than the machine information system.

To learn the craft of Lean management, executives must not attack the human information system with malware (behavioral waste). Doing so would be to learn simple zero-sum conventional management practice, which is not the desired goal.

Instead, executives must do the opposite, which is to eliminate malware from the human information system and constantly defend against it. Only this will be consistent with the "Continuous Improvement" and "Respect for People" principles.

**Notes**

[1] The human information system also includes the information possessed by a company's other key stakeholders: suppliers, customers, investors, and communities. Executives must carefully manage these human information systems as well.

[2] B. Emiliani, *Practical Lean Leadership: A Strategic Leadership Guide for Executives*, The CLBM, LLC, Wethersfield, Conn., 2008

[3] Favoring certain departments or groups of people over others is tremendously short-sighted and destructive. It inflates the egos of people in the in-groups, marginalizes the people in the out-groups, and thus undercuts teamwork. Think of the different departments in a company as the major organs in the human body. It makes no sense to favor certain organs over other; you need all of them in order to function properly.

[4] B. Emiliani, *REAL LEAN: The Keys to Sustaining Lean Management*, Volume Three, The CLBM. LLC, Wethersfield, Conn., 2008

[5] Senior managers almost never perform simple root cause analyses to determine the true source of management problems, despite the fact that most have been trained in how to use the tools (e.g. 5 Whys or fishbone diagram). For the last 10 years I have asked some 1,500 of my graduate students (who work full-time for a living) if any have had an executive show them their own root cause analysis of a management problem. The answer is exactly 1. One student said that a vice president shared with his team a root cause analysis that he did of a problem that plagued the group. This supports the observation that senior managers guess at what causes problems, and therefore also must guess at potential solutions.

[6] To learn more about the intersection of the human information system and organizational capability building, see T. Fujimoto, *The Evolution of a Manufacturing System at Toyota*, Oxford University Press, New York, NY, 1999

[7] The synergies that executives seek from mergers rarely materialize. Both mergers and acquisitions often suffer from serious integration problems and usually have below average share price growth for several years. The parent company is often stuck paying for legacy problems of the divested company, often for many years after the divestiture (e.g. General Motors divestiture of Delphi Corporation).

[8] The list of corporations and corporate officers who have gamed their financial reports in order to show growth never stops growing. A few examples from this past decade include: Enron, Computer Associates, Bristol-Myers Squibb, Thomas & Betts, Sunbeam, Rite-Aid, etc. See

http://www.sec.gov/litigation/litreleases.shtml

[9] Business was created by people to serve the social and economic needs of people.

[10] Explicit knowledge is knowledge documented in the form of work instructions, procedures, etc. – the "science." Tacit knowledge is knowledge that is unspoken, implied, or learned through experience – the "tricks of the trade" or the "art."

# 8 One Step Forward, Eleven Back

*What manager does not cry for more teamwork? For better teamwork? What they seek is people working together to achieved shared goals. To do so requires cooperation and selflessness among team members. This is very difficult to achieve, and often made even more difficult when managers do things that undercut teamwork.*

Executives who want to learn the craft of Lean management have to accept the importance of teamwork – real teamwork, not fake teamwork. They have to model the teamwork beliefs, behaviors, and competencies that they expect to see in other employees. Executive compensation must not be based on department-specific metrics. Instead, it must be based on company metrics and overall corporate performance. Metrics that promote batch-and-queue thinking and practices must be modified, de-emphasized, or eliminated. And, they must become selfless promoters of a customer-first policy, and not promoters of a bunch of separate me-first and my-department-first policies. The executive team itself must exhibit exemplary teamwork that others can learn from. This is one step forward.

Being a good role model is important, but there is much more that executives must do to enable and improve teamwork throughout the company. First, they must answer some questions such as:

- "Do we do things that make it difficult for employees to be effective team members?"

- "Are any of our policies, metrics, or practices at odds with promoting teamwork?"
- "What else might interfere with teamwork?"

Executives who ask these questions will find that there are many ways in which teamwork can be undercut, often inadvertently [1]. Here are some examples:

### 1. Separating Employees by Function

Physically separating employees into different locations by function or discipline is classic batch-and-queue information processing, which slows response times and leads to many errors and rework. Putting all the finance people together in one building, all the engineering people in another building (or state or country), and all the sales and marketing people in yet another location is like putting all the milling machines together in one place, all the lathes together in another place, and all the grinding machines somewhere else.

Separating employees by function can indicate to them that they may not need to interact with people in other departments to any great extent. At the very least, it can introduce ambiguity regarding management's true expectation for cross-functional cooperation. If teamwork is so important, then why isn't the team together?

Dispersing the workforce makes communication and collaboration more difficult. Of course, being co-located does not guarantee effective teamwork just as being far apart does not guarantee ineffective teamwork. However, co-location improves the opportunities for cooperation, collaboration, and, ultimately, teamwork.

2. Favoritism in Who Gets Promoted

If we're the boss, we generally like to promote people who are in our own image, which we tend to think is a pretty good example of what it takes to succeed. While we hear a lot of talk about meritocracies and merit-based promotions, the reality is that merit is not a big factor in many promotion decisions. So, when management says merit is important, yet many of those who get promoted appear to lack merit, then that creates many problems.

One problem is that workers will view the promotion process as unfair. They will rationalize: "Why should I work so hard when there seems to be no benefit?" Predictably, workers are less committed to teamwork under such circumstances.

If managers say merit is important for advancement, then they must advance people who have done work that most people would easily recognize as meritorious. While it is difficult to completely eliminate favoritism, it must be seen by others as an insignificant factor, and, in fact, be insignificant.

Similarly, if managers talk teamwork, then financial and non-financial rewards must predominately go to teams and not to individuals. Exemplary individual performance in the correct application of Lean principles and practices should, of course, be rewarded.

3. Favoring Certain Departments Over Others

It is common for the top executive and other senior managers to favor one department over another. Their favorite is probably the discipline in which they were educated or the department they spent the most time in early in their career. They will make many obvious and subtle comments indicating which department(s) they think work harder or contribute more to the company. However, there is great danger in doing this.

Favoring certain departments over others creates in-groups and out-groups, which quickly leads to distracting, internal us-versus-them rivalries. There can be no real teamwork under such circumstances. And people will surely lose sight of the company's customers.

Executives are officers of the *company*, not officers of a department or discipline. Doing things that marginalize certain individuals or groups is bad for the company. Managers must be very careful of what they say and make sure they are broadly inclusive for meetings and other business activities.

It is helpful to think of the different departments in a company as the major organs of the human body. It makes no sense to favor certain organs over other; you need all of them in order to function properly. It is the same in business: You need all departments in order to function properly.

### 4. Permitting Biases and Stereotypes to Exist

Favoring one department over others is just one form of bias that executives can have. There are many more biases, as well as stereotypes, that can undercut teamwork. Some important examples are:

- Limiting upward advancement for women and minorities. Managers may make an assumption that they are not qualified when, in most cases, they do not actually know the specific requirements for the job. Or, there is abnormally wide variation in job responsibilities, which indicates a poor understanding of roles and responsibilities, and forces managers to search for "superstars" – and likely overpay for work that is nearly impossible for any person to do well.

- Limiting cross-functional work opportunities to people who are assumed to be incapable or unqualified. For example, a facilities engineer would most likely not be given an opportunity to work in the marketing department. Such decisions deflate people's ambitions and contribute to their underperformance.

- Having a low opinion of the people, processes, or work done in departments that senior managers are unfamiliar with. For example, shipping and receiving, purchasing, accounts payable, or human resources. Thinking that these people are less intelligent, less committed, or less important [2] is a mistake.

- Criticizing people who have wild ideas or criticizing people who read as being "theoretical" creates a large out-group that will be unwilling to speak up and share new, innovative ideas.

- Favoring quantitative "numbers" people over qualitative people. The numbers don't tell the whole story and the whole story usually can't be told without some numbers. Favoring quants over quals will lead to poor decision-making. Just because something can't be put into a spreadsheet does not mean it is not real. The two capabilities must be balanced.

- Favoring the ideas and opinions of outside experts over inside experts. Ideas and opinions are not like olives, where imported ones are better. Inside experts are much more affordable than outside experts. Outside experts want executives to think they have no inside experts. Ignoring the ideas and opinions of inside experts is a costly mistake.

Senior managers who allow these biases and stereotypes to exist are not fulfilling their duties as officers of the company. The have failed to develop people and greatly underutilize human resources, limit the value proposition for customers, and also limit returns for shareholders. In addition, these biases and stereotypes usually lead to large disparities in pay, which make people feel cheated and can lessen interest in team participation.

### 5. Fake Teams

Since real teamwork is so difficult to achieve, some managers will make a game of teamwork. For example, a manager has an idea that he or she wants to implement and has already figured out most of the details. But the manager needs the stamp of approval from a team to justify the change. So a team is formed to study the problem and make recommendations. Naturally, the team is heading down a path that will lead to the wrong recommendations, so the manager steers the team to the desired pre-determined outcome. After a while, people catch on to the fact that they are being used and become cynical about teamwork. Workers must trust managers and vice versa. Gaming teamwork abuses the trust that workers have in management and disrespects the knowledge and capabilities of team members.

6. Blame Some People and Praise Others

Some departments, such as purchasing or operations are perpetually made the scapegoat for all kinds of problems. Other departments are immune from criticism, such as finance and legal. This condition proves that senior managers never do root cause analysis. Consistently blaming some people and praising others is an unwritten corporate policy to divide people and ensure that real teamwork will never be achieved.

7. Large Pay Disparities

Large disparities in pay within departments, between departments, or between workers and senior managers can cause unwanted distractions. Typically, the people who create problems are paid much more than the people who clean up the messes. That can be a source of irritation that lessens lower-paid people's desire to participate on teams or contribute to teams.

Perhaps a much greater source of problems is when the pay of the top executive is 100-500 times that of entry-level workers. People can accept the boss being paid 30-90 times that of entry-level workers. Beyond that it can become a sore point that makes teamwork more difficult. Big pay for the select few screams out "me-first" to employees who are told by top managers to be selfless team players. The dissonance is very difficult to resolve.

8. Department-Specific Rewards

Most departments held accountable to department-specific metrics. For example, purchasing is often held accountable primarily for price, while the quality department is held accountable to a defects-per-million or similar metric. In this example, purchasing's metric will almost always be at odds with quality's metric, thus undercutting teamwork between people in the two departments.

When a significant portion of executive compensation is derived from achieving department-specific metrics, the executive will surely drive people in his or her department to hit their metric even if it negatively impacts another department. Department-specific financial rewards for achieving certain metrics will further undercut teamwork.

## 9. Charge Numbers

Some departments are funded by overhead budgets while costs in other departments are closely controlled using a confusing array of charge numbers. Let's say an overhead department such as operations encounters a problem that requires the participation of engineers to help correct. If the engineer has no budget to work on such an activity, then they have to contend with the bureaucracy associated with opening new charge numbers and re-allocating budget or requesting new budget. Most engineers avoid doing this, and so they are not able to work with people in operations to quickly resolve the problem. The problem then lingers on for weeks, months, or even years. The charge number system is clearly a barrier to teamwork.

## 10. Outsourcing Work

Outsourcing work that was once done in-house creates new types of interfaces that employees must learn to work with, which takes time. More importantly, the work that was outsourced, particularly to low-wage countries, can implant worries in the heads of the remaining employees that their jobs could be next. They may feel that there is no point in working hard or being a good team member if executives are determined to dismantle the team, department by department [3].

### 11. Zero-Sum

The mindset that there must be winners and losers is zero-sum, and means that one party must win at someone else's expense. The zero-sum mindset is deeply rooted in our social and economic thinking, but is thoroughly anti-Lean and anti-teamwork [4]. It creates discord that extends beyond the enterprise, adds costs, and consumes time [5]. People worry about being the loser, which leads to some unsavory behaviors and will reduce people's willingness to work together. There can be no real teamwork when senior managers think and behave zero-sum.

Executives are not thinking hard enough if they think there must be winners and losers.

These are some of the obvious ways in which teamwork can be undercut by the senior management team, taking teamwork 11 steps backward. No doubt there are many more than these. The lack of teamwork that many senior managers complain about is exactly what you would expect when these problems, and many others like them, can be found in almost every organization.

Unaware of their role in undercutting teamwork, senior managers will typically do the following:

- Periodically hire expensive trainers to teach the workforce about teamwork or how to improve their teamwork skills.

- Call upon higher education to do a better job of preparing future employees for the team environment they will encounter at work.

Both address the symptoms of the problem, and not its root causes.

Furthermore, employers should view themselves as partners with universities in achieving the life-long learning objectives of students/employees. For their part, managers at all levels must view part of their job as teachers and become good examples of people who read and write, do root cause (non-numerical) analysis, etc., to expand their knowledge for work activities and for their own personal benefit.

The path to learning the craft of Lean management begins with executives who ask fundamental questions and then take action to eliminate inconsistencies:

- "Do we do things that make it difficult for employees to be effective team members?"
- "Are any of our policies, metrics, or practices at odds with promoting teamwork?"
- "What else might interfere with teamwork?"

**Notes**

[1] It is inadvertent to the extent that executives don't think to ask these questions. Yet it is also deliberate to the extent that executives don't ask these questions.

[2] The CEO of brewer InBev NV, Carlos Brito, had this to say about which InBev employees are important and which are not: "Mr. Brito told the Stanford [business school] audience that out of InBev's 85,000 employees, only 200 to 250 'are really the ones who make a difference.' He said InBev is unapologetic about giving special treatment to the difference makers." The other 84,750 employees are probably not happy, but who cares... they don't make a difference. "InBev's Chief Built Competitive Culture," by M. Moffett, *The Wall Street Journal*, 13 June 2008.

[3] Local suppliers are also part of the team that management often seeks to dismantle to obtain lower unit prices on purchased goods and services – but often at higher total costs.

[4] B. Emiliani, *REAL LEAN: The Keys to Sustaining Lean Management,* Volume Three, The CLBM, LLC, Wethersfield, Conn., 2008

[5] Losers, unhappy with their position, try to get even and will eventually succeed – usually at winners' expense. Zero-sum thinking has costs that always work against winners' interests.

# 9 The Ethical Management System

*Most businesses strive to operate to the highest ethical standards. Whether there are 10 employees or 100,000 or more, all are expected to conduct business activities in accordance with corporate codes of ethics. The question that people do not consider is: What is the relationship between the management system that executives use and business ethics? Can the management system make it easier or more difficult for employees to conform to corporate codes of ethics?*

Recall in Chapter 3 that Teruyuki Minoura, former president of Toyota Motor Manufacturing North America, said [1]:

> "When I reflect on what Mr. Ohno taught us, one thing that stands out to me is that he taught us how to think. He taught us to think deeply. When I think about this, I think that perhaps the 'T' in TPS should stand not only for Toyota, but also for 'Thinking.' The 'Thinking Production System'."

In fact, Toyota's overall management system is a "Thinking Management System" because it requires people to think in ways they have never done before. In this chapter, we're going to think about ethics in ways we have not thought of before: the relationship between ethics and the management systems that executives use.

Broadly speaking, businesses are managed by executives in one of two ways: zero-sum (win-lose) or non-zero-sum (win-win). Primitive zero-sum management, where one party gains at someone else's expense, is by far the most common way to manage a business. Non-zero-sum management is much rarer, in part because it requires senior managers to think, unlearn some things, and learn many new things. It is the fundamental idea behind Toyota's management practice.

Ethics is important to all businesses, but especially to global corporations with reputations, brands, and sales volumes to safeguard. The words typically used to characterize ethical business practices include: fairness, trust, communication, respect, responsibility, integrity, stakeholders, good faith, relationships, communities, dignity, and so on. To help avoid ethical lapses, corporations spend large sums of money on periodic ethics training for employees and develop internal processes for reporting and investigating suspected violations. These are good things to do. But how effective are they? Is ethics operating at a six-sigma level of quality or better in large corporations?

I think the answer is "no," because managers typically do not engage in root cause analysis to understand the true source of problems, ethical or otherwise. So ethics problems are likely to be repeated periodically, in the case of severe problems, and perhaps much more frequently depending upon how the word "ethics" is defined. We will use the dictionary definition of the word "ethics" [2]:

"A set of principles of right conduct."

My premise is a simple one: that ethics training will be less effective in companies where top management's dominant view and practice of business is zero-sum, because zero-sum is not "right conduct" for business. Nowhere is business defined as having to be zero-sum, yet that is the way it is most often practiced by executives and should lead to recurring ethics problems.

To put it bluntly, screwing your employees, suppliers, customers, communities, and yes, even investors, is not "right conduct." Screwing your key stakeholders once is not "right conduct," and screwing them again and again is not "right conduct." It creates people who want to work against you, or at least won't work as hard for you. And most employees do what their leaders do.

Which adage do you think more executives subscribe to when it comes to business?

"Do unto others before they do unto you"
*or*
"Do unto others as you wish be done to you."

Most, but certainly not all, subscribe to the former, some to the latter, and some to both. For those who subscribe to both, the former adage likely prevails in tough times.

Zero-sum thinking promotes "wrong conduct," and you don't learn the craft of Lean management through wrong conduct [3]. Wrong conduct means managers at all levels make zero-sum tradeoffs between key stakeholders: employees, suppliers, customers, investors, and communities. The table lists some of the major zero-sum actions that are commonly taken by managers.

| Stakeholder | Common Zero-Sum Actions |
|---|---|
| Employees | Limit growth of pay to below inflation; reduce employee benefits; maintain male-female wage gap; unpaid "casual" overtime; outsource work to low-wage countries; layoff people who helped achieve productivity gains; excessive use of part-time labor; ignore employee suggestions; layoff people for management's errors. |
| Suppliers | Coerce suppliers to lower prices; use new zero-sum tools such as reverse auctions to drive prices downward; threaten to move the work if suppliers do not comply with customer's demands; refuse to accept legitimate price increases (e.g. raw material, energy); paying suppliers late; extending payment terms from 30 to 75 days; unilaterally debit suppliers' account payable for unresolved problems; fine suppliers for mistakes; bid shopping; not honoring terms and conditions of trade. |
| Customers | Sell defective products and services; don't listen to the voice of the customer; use deceptive advertising to increase sales; reducing customer service and support to cut costs; price-fixing; channel stuffing, tying. |
| Investors | Limit growth by not listening to customers; excessive spending on executive pay and perquisites; inflating earnings; channel stuffing; failure to disclose information that is material to investor's interests; insider trading; stock option backdating; dismantle shareholder's assets. |
| Communities | Close facilities; pollute air, land, and water; delay, defer, or avoid paying taxes; abandon properties; underpayment of royalties. |

The irony is that most of the trade-offs are done by senior management to satisfy investors' interests, yet they often end up hurting investors' interests. "Wrong conduct" creates confusion, contradictions, and conflicts that negatively impact every stakeholder and results in ethics problems. It is impossible to be ethical operating a zero-sum management system rife with shortcuts, and it is also the most resource-intensive way to run a business [4].

Here is a real-world example, simplified a bit, to illustrate how a typical large, conventionally managed company, uses an unethical zero-sum tactic to reduce costs and creates other ethics problems. The unethical zero-sum tactic is a new form of supplier price-beating called reverse auctions, which most senior managers like to use because they think it saves a lot of money quickly [5].

> ABC durable goods company in East Hartford, Conn., buys machined parts from SZY supplier in New Britain, Conn., for many years. After the reverse auction, SZY supplier loses the work to PAT supplier in India because they have much lower unit prices due to lower labor costs. ABC agrees to purchase the products from PAT supplier, located over 7000 miles away. Now the raw material, made in Pennsylvania, must be purchased by ABC and shipped to PAT in India, and the finished part is shipped from India to East Hartford (more time and more money).

> The mode of transport of the raw material to India, and of the finished products from India to an eastern U.S. port, is via slow container ships, which increases inventories. And ships are extremely dirty in terms of bilge waste and high in carbon dioxide and particulate emissions.

There is a 100 percent probability that there will be part shortages, which will require product to be shipped via air cargo. Airplanes engines produce large amounts of carbon dioxide and nitrous oxide emissions. The parts have to pass through customs (a delay) and get trucked from a New York airport to East Hartford (diesel fuel and more time, plus trucking expedite charges).

In contrast, the amount of carbon dioxide emitted from local sourcing is tiny a fraction of that emitted when products are sourced globally. SZY supplier gets their raw material from Pennsylvania once a week, performs the work, and then delivers the product using a small van traveling from New Britain to East Hartford – a distance of 14 miles that takes 30 minutes and consumes about 2 gallons of gasoline round-trip.

What ABC company has done is trade a Connecticut labor price of $20 per hour for Indian labor at $5 per hour. That seems like a really good deal. But it takes SZY supplier only 2-20 labor hours to make most of the parts in the commodity category that was sourced to India (less than 50 percent value added). PAT supplier needs 10-50 labor hours or more to produce the same parts, which erodes some of the labor cost advantage, as do the inventories and logistics costs.

The ethical problems that have been created by trying to reduce the unit price of purchased materials, in order to reduce the cost of goods sold and increase cash flow, are as follows:

- Apply zero-sum price reduction tactic to incumbent

supplier, in violation of corporate ethics statement for dealing with suppliers.

- Commitments to customers are broken due to late deliveries and quality problems.
- Global sourcing is inconsistent with ABC company's efforts to reduce its environmental footprint.
- ABC company contributes to environmental damage but is not responsible for it; communities will some-day have to pay.
- The total cost items purchased is higher, thus increasing the cost of goods sold at shareholder's expense.
- Increased costs means some ABC employees will have to be laid off.

The message is simple: zero-sum tactics increase costs and create ethical (and other) problems for the company and its stakeholders. ABC company should have continued to buy locally and addressed high labor costs by working with SZY supplier to understand the root cause of cost problems and identify practical countermeasures. A different, mutually beneficial business opportunity could be pursued with PAT supplier that has less negative impacts on other stakeholders and the environment.

Primitive zero-sum conventional management will naturally lead to many ethical problems because it lacks the principles, concepts, practices, methods and tools to avoid them. It has:

- No clearly stated corporate purpose (reason for exis-tence) [6].
- No business principles to guide management thinking and decision-making [6].

- Oblivious to waste, unevenness, and unreasonableness.
- Uses metrics that drive people to game the measures to achieve the numbers even if it causes other types of problems.
- Organizational politics and wasteful leadership behaviors seen as normal and assumed to have zero cost.
- Indifferent to understanding details of business processes.
- Results-focused.
- Unresponsive to fairness.
- Zero-sum toolkit.

Lean management, on the other hand, has:

- Clearly stated corporate purpose (reason for existence).
- Business principles to guide management thinking and decision-making, "Continuous Improvement" and "Respect for People."
- Great awareness of waste, unevenness, and unreasonableness.
- Uses simple metrics that connect processes.
- Organizational politics and wasteful leadership behaviors seen as abnormal and known to be very expensive.
- Concerned about understanding details of business processes.
- Focused on process and results.
- Seeks to ensure fairness.
- Non-zero-sum toolkit.

To be sure, Lean management is not the perfect management system, and ethical problems can and do occur periodically. But the frequency and severity of such events is diminished because of its principles, concepts, practices, methods and tools, which people adhere to because it is more logical and respectful of people compared to the alternatives.

Therefore, executives who are committed to ethics would be wise to abandon primitive zero-sum conventional management. Adopting Lean management would be more consistent with the ethical and myriad other business objectives that executives seek to achieve without having to rely on selfishness, financial engineering, and bad leadership behaviors [7] to get the job done.

This chapter provided some basic insights into the relationship between the management system that executives use and business ethics. Conventional zero-sum management makes it more difficult for employees to conform to corporate codes of ethics. Lean management makes it easier for employees to conform to corporate codes of ethics because it rejects screwing the company's stakeholders as a primary means to succeed.

Perhaps the most challenging aspect of learning the craft of Lean management is for executives to abandon their zero-sum mindset and practices because it is so deeply ingrained after decades of work experience [8]. Most executives can see no other way to win than by using zero-sum tactics [9]. Instead, executives must adopt the non-zero-sum mindset and practices and win with them.

This leadership transformation is necessary but not sufficient to create Lean leaders and a Lean business. The executive team must systematically de-emphasize, modify, or eliminate policies, metrics, practices, and processes that are zero-sum in every department. They must closely scrutinize how they deal with employees, suppliers, customers, investors, communities, and even competitors to eliminate non-zero-sum actions and behaviors. They must also change the reward system for teams and individuals who correctly apply Lean principles and practices.

Lean management is not only the "Thinking Management System," it is also the "Ethical Management System." Knowing this, how can you justify remaining committed to less ethical zero-sum conventional management?

Notes

[1] T. Minoura, "Address to the World Class Manufacturing Forum," May 2002,http://www.electronics-scotland.com/industry_comment/comment_item.cfm?itemID=18

[2] *The American Heritage College Dictionary*, 3rd edition, Houghton Mifflin Co., New York, 1997, p. 471

[3] That would be like learning the craft of woodworking by cutting boards transversely when they need to be cut lengthwise. It's the wrong way to do it.

[4] Let's say you are genetically incapable of thinking of business in any way other than financial. So consider a business to be a gold mine. Conventional management practices extract only 70 percent of the gold from the ore. Tweaking the existing process will eventually improve the yield to 79-80 percent. That's a significant improvement, but an enormous amount on money is lost. To get 95 percent yield or better, you have to switch to a completely new process that requires new ways of thinking and doing the work. The new process will require some investment of time and money, but will obviously yield big returns to those willing to learn. Sadly, most managers are not willing to learn.

[5] In most cases the unit price savings from reverse auctions is an illusion, quality problems and delays are common, and total costs increase. See "REVERSE AUCTIONS: A Ten Year Research Project Investigating Business-to-Business Reverse Auctions," M.L. "Bob" Emiliani, http://www.technology.ccsu.edu/personnel/information/emiliani/ra_research.html

[6] "Maximize shareholder value" is not a bona-fide corporate purpose. See B. Emiliani, *REAL LEAN: The Keys to Sustaining Lean Management,* Volume Three, The CLBM, LLC, Wethersfield, Conn., 2008

[7] Corporate leaders often exhibit sub-criminal psychopathic behaviors such as: exaggerated sense of self worth, manipulative, lack of empathy for the feelings of other people, lack of remorse, failure to accept responsibility for errors, etc. They behave this way to control other people. We abhor physical ownership of people (slavery), but it seems we do not abhor mental ownership of people through the use of fear, threats, coercion, intimidation, etc. These behaviors are the stock-in-trade of sub-criminal psychopaths. The conventional zero-sum management system is a safe harbor for these types of "leaders." It is not ethical, and likely immoral, for boards of directors to permit the existence of a defective management system that attracts this type of person to the highest levels of management.

[8] It might be helpful for some to view zero-sum as a large tax on a busi-

ness, caused by the copious amounts of conflict, distrust, tit-for-tat, and other wasteful behaviors. Non-zero-sum is not tax-free, but it is a much smaller tax on a business than zero-sum because behavioral waste is greatly diminished. You can reduce your internal corporate tax by adopting non-zero-sum Lean management.

[9] The following quote from *The Wall Street Journal* article titled "ECO:nomics: Creating Environmental Capital" (24 March 2008, p. R1) illustrates how ingrained zero-sum thinking is in business: "The push to curb global-warming emissions is starting to redraw the industrial landscape, and in doing so it has already begun to create new winners and losers. Job One for a CEO is: Exploit the opportunities and shift the costs to someone else."

# 10 Policies for Learning

*Learning the craft of Lean management means the doors
to learning must be thrown wide-open and all barriers
removed. Supporting people's efforts to learn Lean
management is not enough. Executives must do specific
things to help themselves and others learn in
order to enable the Lean culture to emerge.*

Culture change is a common objective that senior management decides is necessary in order for the company to meet future business challenges that are materially different than past business challenges. Everybody acknowledges culture change as the major challenge when a company embarks on a Lean transformation. Since culture is so important, let's define it. Culture is [1]:

> "The beliefs and assumptions that guide people's thinking and decision making."

Thus, to achieve culture change requires all employees, top to bottom, to embrace new beliefs and assumptions related to their understanding and practice of business.

Too often, however, the people in companies fail to change incrementally in how they think about and do work and are then suddenly faced with having to make big changes all at once. Figure 1 illustrates the problem:

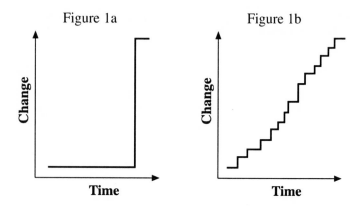

Figure 1a

Figure 1b

In Figure 1a, there is not much change over a long period of time [2]. Then something important happens in the marketplace that requires employees to make drastic changes in how they think about and do things. The company is in trouble and people have to make many big changes fast. A large step-function change is needed, but is extremely difficult to achieve – particularly in big companies. It is like cramming for a test; it usually does not work. But that is what most companies do.

In Figure 1b, employees are making small changes every day in response to daily changes in market conditions. They have not waited for trouble to ignite change. Instead, they adapted to changing circumstances in real time, rather than delaying adaptation (Figure 1a). They rarely have to cram. This is what REAL LEAN companies do.

Executives typically drive culture change by telling people the reasons why change is needed, giving them books to read about the "change or die" imperative, and enrolling them in expensive training programs. However, it is rare that a senior management team will change or modify corporate policies, metrics, or practices, or their own beliefs to help achieve the desired outcomes. They seem to think, incorrectly, that these have no impact on learning and culture change. So while they want employees to change, their ability to change is highly constrained by executives who, paradoxically, maintain the status-quo.

Predictably, the inability of employees to change causes a lot of frustration. Top managers think employees are the problem and often target supervisors and middle managers as they key barriers – without ever doing any root cause analysis. Employees point the finger at senior managers for not "walking the talk" [3] with respect to culture change. The result is stasis, which is not a good situation to be in when the company's future is at risk.

Top executives are officers of the company and can't sit around doing nothing. They will soon have no choice but to take action. They will force the organization to make painful, disruptive changes by taking actions that are directly within their control: management shake-up, reorganize departments, layoffs, acquire a business, spin off a business, merge, etc. Unfortunately, these actions will do nothing to support the emergence of the new desired culture.

The culture change that is sought by executives is a learning process, and learning takes time – just as it has taken time to learn the old way of thinking and doing things. Impatient executives want to see major culture change occur quickly, in one or two years. But that is not going to happen by telling people why they need to change, giving them books to read, or sending them to training classes. Executives want big changes, but they do not think to modify corporate policies, metrics, or practices to enable the changes they seek.

Let's say a major feature of the culture change is to become customer-focused, rather than company-focused. If being customer-focused is the desired outcome, then most metrics that are company-focused, such as earned hours and purchase price variance, should be de-emphasized, modified, or eliminated. But that rarely happens. If customer-focus is the new culture, then an engineer should not have to fight with finance to obtain budget to work with operations to correct a customer's problem. But that rarely happens; the budget is more important than the customer. If customer-focus is so important, then employees should be able to remedy customer complaints without having to get management's permission to do so. But that rarely happens.

These are just a few examples of how the CEOs call for culture change will be blocked by existing company policies, metrics, and practices. Your team can find dozens more, I'm sure.

Companies also have lots of unwritten policies that mostly belong to individual senior managers. These are also huge barriers to changing the culture, but are more insidious because they lurk in the background. Let's explore these in more detail.

A policy is [4]:

> "A course of action, guiding principle, or procedure considered expedient, prudent, or advantageous."

Senior managers' unwritten policies come from the beliefs they have about business, people, money, the way to do work, etc. Let's say a senior manager holds a belief that people are the problem. The boss's personal unwritten policy, then, in most cases, will be to blame people for problems. This is a policy that discourages learning among employees and makes culture change much more difficult to achieve.

Table 1 lists some common management beliefs and the policy, or course of action taken, in response to the belief. The beliefs and policies are grouped into four categories: economic, social, political, and legal. Note that some of the items in the rows could also fit into other categories.

## Table 1 – Beliefs and Policies that Discourage Learning

| Senior Managment Belief | Unwritten Policy |
|---|---|
| **Social** | |
| We know what customers want | Ignore voice of customer and / or customer feedback |
| People are the problem | Blame people for problems |
| Senior managers are smarter than other people | Centralize decision-making among top leaders |
| The real knowledge is at the top of the company | OK to lose knowledge down below (e.g. offshoring work) |
| Continuous improvement is for other people to do | Make others do continuous improvement |
| Unions are bad | Marginalize and denigrate unions and union members |
| Teamwork is good | Advocate teamwork |
| Older workers won't change or adapt | Get rid of older workers |
| **Economic** | |
| Produce to capacity | Supply-side microeconomics |
| Suppliers are screwing us | Force supplier prices downward |
| Trade-offs are necessary | Low cost more important than high quality |
| Continuous improvement is too slow (incrementalism) | Disrupt continuous improvement activities |
| "Business is business" | Marginalize humanity |
| **Political** | |
| Organizational politics is a fact of life | Condone / promote organizational politics |
| Must say the right thing | Say the right things |
| Company is not a democracy | Unilateralism ("my way or the highway") |
| Withhold bad news as long as possible | Spin and obfuscation |
| **Legal** | |
| Shareholders own the company | Focus all efforts to benefit shareholders |
| Liability is limited | Mistakes will be made |
| Must abide by code of ethics | Must be very aggressive to get things done |
| It's my business to know that, not yours | Tightly control information to key internal and external stakeholders (e.g. suppliers) |

The culture change that top executives seek will never be achieved with these unwritten policies.

Manager's beliefs have to change before the unwritten policies can change. If this cannot be done, then employees – including supervisors and middle managers – will not risk learning the new culture. Their day-to-day work life, income, rewards, etc., are too dependent on their boss's unwritten policies, to which they must conform.

Let's say the culture change that management desires is to become a Lean company. Senior managers who possess the beliefs and unwritten policies shown in Table 1 will surely fail in their Lean transformation. Instead, they have to possess the beliefs and unwritten policies shown in Table 2. As I have said repeatedly in this and other volumes of *REAL LEAN*, kaizen is the principal process for changing senior managers' beliefs [5].

## Table 2 – Beliefs and Policies that Encourage Learning

| Senior Managment Belief | Unwritten Policy |
|---|---|
| **Social** ||
| We don't know what customers want | Listen to voice of customer and customer feedback |
| People are not the problem | Improve processes |
| Senior managers are not smarter than other people | Decentralize decision-making to where the work is done |
| The real knowledge is not at the top of the company | Retain worker's knowledge |
| Continuous improvement is for everyone | Participate in continuous improvement |
| Unions are not bad | Work with union to achieve shared objectives |
| Teamwork is good | Participate in teams |
| Older workers can change or adapt | Utilize older workers |
| **Economic** ||
| Produce to customer demand | Demand-side microeconomics |
| Suppliers are our partners | Work with suppliers to understand and correct problems |
| Trade-offs are not necessary | Low cost and high quality are important |
| Continuous improvement is what we do every day | Participate in continuous improvement activities |
| "Business is human" | Respect humanity |
| **Political** ||
| Organizational politics is not a fact of life | Reduce / eliminate organizational politics |
| Must know what you're talking about | Go see for yourself |
| Company is partly a democracy | Embrace democratic principles |
| Disclose bad news as soon as possible | Get the facts and clarify |
| **Legal** ||
| Shareholders are one of five key stakeholders | Must balance interests of all key stakeholders |
| Liability is limited | Mistakes should be avoided and not repeated |
| Must abide by code of ethics | Don't get close to the line. |
| It's our business to know that | Share relevant information with key internal and external stakeholders (e.g. suppliers) |

Senior managers who possess these beliefs and unwritten policies pave the way for workers to learn Lean management, which then begins the process of culture change in earnest. Importantly, consistency in executive's beliefs and daily application of the policies shown in Table 2 will accelerate culture change company-wide [6].

**Notes**

[1] B. Emiliani, *Practical Lean Leadership: A Strategic Leadership Guide for Executives*, The CLBM, LLC, Wethersfield, Conn., 2008, p. 70

[2] The image in Figure 1a implies that no change is occurring, which is not entirely accurate. There are changes occurring, but slowly and not of any great significance, which is why a sudden major change in culture will eventually be required.

[3] Using the phrase "walk the walk" instead of "walk the talk" proves someone is not thinking.

[4] *The American Heritage College Dictionary*, 3rd edition, Houghton Mifflin Co., New York, 1997, p. 1058

[5] B. Emiliani, *Practical Lean Leadership: A Strategic Leadership Guide for Executives*, The CLBM, LLC, Wethersfield, Conn., 2008

[6] A word to the wise: Do not chase the rainbow and think that one day you will have learned Lean management or that the new culture will someday stick. Just keep on learning Lean management. See B. Emiliani, *REAL LEAN: The Keys to Sustaining Lean Management*, Volume Three, The CLBM, LLC, Wethersfield, Conn., 2008

# 11 Eleven Questions

This Volume of REAL LEAN informs readers that it is quite a challenge to learn the Lean management system, but also explains why it is worthwhile for executives to do so. A big part of the challenge is to learn that Lean principles and practices do not stand alone.

Indeed, Lean principles and practices are closely interconnected, which few people realize. These interconnections are like woven cloth; some are rather obvious while many others are very subtle or are nuanced which only a master craftsperson would know. It is these interconnections that make Lean management so fun and interesting to learn.

Below are 11 questions to sharpen your awareness of the interconnections that exist between Lean principles and practices. The specific focus of the questions is the relationship between continuous improvement tools and processes and the "Respect for People" principle.

This relationship is important for students of Lean management to understand generally, but more so in the context of the interests of each one of the five key stakeholders: employees, suppliers, customers, investors, and communities. This will help you develop a much deeper understanding of the non-zero-sum nature of Lean management.

You will know Lean management pretty well when you can answer all 11 of these questions (requiring more than 55 answers). But don't be satisfied with that. These are just a small sample of the many interconnections. There is always more to learn.

---

### **Instructions**

Please fill in your answers to each of the following
11 questions for each category of stakeholder.
There may be more than one answer in each category
of stakeholder. You should do this over the course
of many months or years as you learn
more about Lean management.

---

Question 1. How does takt time (the rate of customer demand) demonstrate "Respect for People" for each one of the five key stakeholders?

• Employees

• Suppliers

• Customers

• Investors

• Communities

Question 2. How does standardized work demonstrate "Respect for People" for each one of the five key stakeholders?

• Employees

• Suppliers

• Customers

• Investors

• Communities

Question 3. How does root cause analysis demonstrate "Respect for People" for each one of the five key stakeholders?

• Employees

• Suppliers

• Customers

• Investors

• Communities

Question 4. How does heijunka (level loading) demonstrate "Respect for People" for each one of the five key stakeholders?

• Employees

• Suppliers

• Customers

• Investors

• Communities

Question 5. How does jidoka (autonomation) demonstrate "Respect for People" for each one of the five key stakeholders?

• Employees

• Suppliers

• Customers

• Investors

• Communities

Question 6. How does Just-in-Time demonstrate "Respect for People" for each one of the five key stakeholders?

• Employees

• Suppliers

• Customers

• Investors

• Communities

Question 7. How does set-up reduction demonstrate "Respect for People" for each one of the five key stakeholders?

• Employees

• Suppliers

• Customers

• Investors

• Communities

Question 8. How does kanban demonstrate "Respect for People" for each one of the five key stakeholders?

• Employees

• Suppliers

• Customers

• Investors

• Communities

Question 9. How does mistake-proofing demonstrate "Respect for People" for each one of the five key stakeholders?

• Employees

• Suppliers

• Customers

• Investors

• Communities

Question 10. How do visual controls demonstrate "Respect for People" for each one of the five key stakeholders?

• Employees

• Suppliers

• Customers

• Investors

• Communities

Question 11. How does kaizen demonstrate "Respect for People" for each one of the five key stakeholders?

• Employees

• Suppliers

• Customers

• Investors

• Communities

# 12 Emiliani's Twelve Rules

Executives learning the craft of Lean management should follow these 12 rules:

| | |
|---|---|
| Rule 1: | Flow on a micro- or macro-scale is achieved only when self-interest is satisfied or removed. |
| Rule 2: | "Respect for People" principle is required, not optional [1]. |
| Rule 3: | Kaizen is the principal learning process. |
| Rule 4: | Effort must be continuous – practice every day. |
| Rule 5: | Application must be broad-based; no person or department is exempt from learning and participation. |
| Rule 6: | All managers must have cross-functional work experiences [2]. |
| Rule 7: | Thinking and doing must be balanced. |
| Rule 8: | Question everything – ask "Why?" [3]. |
| Rule 9: | Spend ideas, not dollars [4]. |
| Rule 10: | Make most changes rapidly. |
| Rule 11: | Read, study, and try new things [5]. |
| Rule 12: | Have fun. |

Remember, Lean management is 80 percent tacit knowledge and 20 percent explicit knowledge – the opposite of what you are used to.

**Notes**

[1] Includes a no-blame policy and no layoffs due to kaizen policy.

[2] Executives must not be lifetime functional specialists. And, they must apply Lean principles and practices in each cross-functional work experience.

[3] Ask "Why?" to ensure consistency with Lean principles and practices: corporate purpose, metrics, performance appraisal process, compensation and rewards, etc.

[4] Told to Emiliani by sensei Yoshihisa Doi in 1994.

[5] Read and study to gain an accurate understanding of Lean principles and practices. Be careful to screen out the large amount of bad information.

# *Afterword*

This volume brings Lean full circle. Lean management is the evolutionary product of progressive management principles and practices that were created to move away from late 1800s craft production into mass production and beyond – beyond the need to rely on scale.

I wanted to devote a volume that highlighted how Lean management is itself a craft. Few people understand it in that context, including the best Lean practitioners and Lean thinkers (external to Toyota). That is because most leaders think that management, in general, is a relatively simple activity that they can improvise their way through. Thinking of management this way is the antithesis of craft, and helps explain why mediocre management is the norm.

Viewing Lean management as a craft creates a different impression of what executives need to do. It informs them that their learning must be much deeper than they might have imagined. It means that executives have a lot of work to do. Fortunately, the learning occurs in small steps: the daily development of Lean thinking and Lean doing skills. With each passing week you will see yourself progress. After just a year you'll be amazed at all that you've learned and how much better the business functions. And so it goes, year after year – if you remain committed.

You will face a serious self-imposed threat to becoming a Lean leader: certitude. Certitude is a liability when it comes to Lean because it is the death of ideas, trying new things, and learning. The problem that teachers have long had in educating senior managers about Lean is that they are certain they already know it. They don't. Neither do the teachers.

With Lean management, you are learning something completely new and different. You may know how to play the trumpet very well, but now you are learning to play the piano. While some general musicianship skills will carry over, the two instruments are otherwise completely different. Despite your years of experience, you are a beginner again.

Almost every executive is tripped-up by the "Respect for People" principle. They are certain they know what it means, but they are wrong. To avoid making the same mistake, you should assume you do not at all understand what the "Respect for People" principle means. Only then you might actually begin to learn what it means.

Various teachers will help you learn Lean management in-person, online, and on paper (such as this book). The teacher facilitates learning, but ultimately it is you who must take full responsibility for learning. If you are motivated to learn, then you will soon realize that much of what you were taught in college and by past supervisors is in need of both major and minor revision. Some people are troubled by this because they are convinced that their teachers did a great job teaching them how to think and gave them accurate and useful information.

The reality is that if you never came across formal root cause analysis in college or graduate school, then you can be assured that your teachers did not teach you how to think. And, if you were taught root cause analysis in industry and have not used what you were taught, then you can be assured that you did not teach yourself how to think. Also, don't be fooled; lots of inaccurate and not-so-useful information gets recycled over the years in both academic and business settings.

When it comes to learning Lean management, you start as a student and quickly evolve into both teacher and student. You teach yourself as well as others, and you are forever a student who learns from others. It is mostly up to you to teach yourself how to think and obtain accurate and useful information. Most people find this liberating because they begin to see things much more clearly and become better managers and leaders.

Welcome to the craft.

*"That isn't how I taught you to do it..."*

## About the Author

 M.L. "Bob" Emiliani is a professor at Connecticut State University in New Britain, Conn., where he teaches various courses on Lean management.

He worked in the consumer products and aerospace industries for nearly two decades and held management positions in engineering, manufacturing, and supply chain management, and had responsibility for implementing Lean in manufacturing operations and supply chains.

Emiliani has authored or co-authored a dozen papers related to Lean leadership including: "Lean Behaviors" (1998), "Linking Leaders' Beliefs to their Behaviors and Competencies" (2003), "Using Value Stream Maps to Improve Leadership" (2004), "Origins of Lean Management in America: The Role of Connecticut Businesses" (2006), and "Standardized Work for Executive Leadership" (2008). Five of his papers have won awards for excellence.

He is the principal author of the book *Better Thinking, Better Results: Case Study and Analysis of an Enterprise-Wide Lean Transformation*, (second edition, 2007), a detailed case study and analysis of The Wiremold Company's Lean transformation from 1991 to 2001. It won a Shingo Research Prize in 2003 as the first book to describe an enterprise-wide Lean transformation in a real company where both principles of Lean management – "Continuous Improvement" and "Respect for People" – were applied.

He is also the author of *REAL LEAN: Understanding the Lean Management System* (Volume One) and *REAL LEAN: Critical Issues and Opportunities in Lean Management* (Volume Two), both published in 2007, *REAL LEAN: The Keys to Sustaining Lean Management* (Volume Three), published in 2008, and *Practical Lean Leadership: A Strategic Leadership Guide For Executives*, published in 2008.

Emiliani holds engineering degrees from the University of Miami, the University of Rhode Island, and Brown University.

He is the owner of The Center for Lean Business Management, LLC. (www.theclbm.com).

Printed in the United Kingdom
by Lightning Source UK Ltd.
136074UK00001B/47/P